It's Never Too Late

Trudy Nuñez Montoya

ISBN 979-8-88540-894-3 (paperback)
ISBN 979-8-89043-977-2 (hardcover)
ISBN 979-8-88540-895-0 (digital)

Copyright © 2023 by Trudy Nuñez Montoya

All rights reserved. No part of this publication may be reproduced, distributed, or transmitted in any form or by any means, including photocopying, recording, or other electronic or mechanical methods without the prior written permission of the publisher. For permission requests, solicit the publisher via the address below.

Christian Faith Publishing
832 Park Avenue
Meadville, PA 16335
www.christianfaithpublishing.com

Printed in the United States of America

CHAPTER 1

The Good Ole Times

My name is Trudy Nunez Montoya, and I want to share my story.

Growing up out in the country was the best. We ran around outside barefoot, climbed trees, and jumped down houses and barns. We made tree swings and clubhouses. We built go-carts and took apart radios and clocks just to put them back together. We rode bikes and played hide-and-go-seek. We played slip 'n' slide with my daddy's blue tarp and four bricks to hold down the corners and played football. We played basketball and baseball, and I played with dolls. I had a Rainbow Brite, My Little Pony, Cabbage Patch Kids, and a few Barbies.

We ate rice, beans, and macaroni. I even ate my Fruity Pebbles with orange juice once because we had no milk. We bathed with a hot bucket of water heated on the stove. All I knew was life was great! When you're young, you didn't get involved with adult discussions. You were always sent to another room, but I always made sure to be close enough to be able to hear them. When I was around seven or eight years old, a cousin of mine who was older than me came to visit my grandma and grandpa who lived next door. We invited her to spend the night at our house so we could play. Later that night, we took a shower together. She touched me and encouraged me to touch her. After we were done bathing, we slept in the same bed, and she began to touch me again as we lay in my bed. She told me not to tell anyone, so I didn't.

Sometime around 1988, I came home from school and saw *After School Special* on television. As I was watching this show, I realized I needed to tell my parents what had happened to me a few years back.

I knew after watching that program that I needed to speak up about my cousin molesting me. I ran to tell my mother what happened to me years ago while my cousin had spent the night. I told her how she touched me. My mom then told my dad when he got home from work. My mother said that my grandmother couldn't know about this, that it would hurt her too bad. My grandmother would be devastated to know her son's daughter molested me.

(Crying inside) But, what about me? What about me! Am I not worth protecting? Am I not worth defending! What about me! I am a child. Love me. Hold me. Tell me everything is going to be okay. Tell my cousin what she did to me wasn't okay! Do something! But instead, it was swept under the rug, hidden, pretending that it never happened. But I couldn't pretend. Those images haunted me as I grew up. A resentment toward my mother started there, not realizing that demons of anger and hatred were inside me—a demon of unforgiveness too. And they were working inside me, destroying me, and playing with my emotions and thoughts.

My dad always worked since he was in the eighth grade. After he got married to my mom, he worked at a cement company, drove trucks and dump trucks, then worked for the city of Alvin, then transferred to the city of Pearland. He would go to work all day just to come home and cut the grass. He was that way. My mom says he doesn't know how to sit down. My father was a hardworking man who loved his family and did what he had to, making sure we had a roof over our head, food to eat, and clothes to wear.

He would come home some days and play with Rudy, Gabriel, and me. He would wrestle us, tickle us, and try to pinch us with his big toe. Back then, children were the remote controller for the TV. It wasn't fun when you were the one chosen to search for a movie or show to watch.

Mom was either working outside in the yard, drawing, sewing, or practicing singing. My parents would rent a table at the Pearland flea market to do resale on the weekends for extra money. My brothers and I would sell some of our toys so we could make some money too. We would end up going around the flea market and buy some more toys—too funny. My grandparents Ricardo "Popo" and Rafaela "Nana" would do resell as well. It was something our family did to earn extra income to make sure all of our needs were met; plus, I think we all enjoyed the business aspect of it.

Back at "The Ranch" where we lived, Popo had a barn, and we did too. They were full of tools, wood, lawnmowers, cow heads, tires, all kinds of stuff we kids could play with, without permission, of course. We would go in there and build stuff or take stuff apart. We would try to build clubhouses and ramps for our bikes. We lived out in the country, us, Popo, Nana, and Oscar, my cousin. Oscar lived with my grandparents; he had been with them since he was a young boy.

Living out in the country is awesome. We ran around barefoot and stayed out until dark. There are no close neighbors. Whenever my aunts and uncles would come to visit Popo and Nana, well, of course, all our cousins would come too! We would have a field day. We were all so close back then. We each had a favorite cousin, mine was Moses. I loved him so much. We all got along so well together—all the cousins. We had a secret language none of the adults could understand.

My brothers and I were close. We played games together and played outside together. I love my baby brothers. I feel like I helped raise my littlest brother Gabriel like a son. I helped a whole lot with him, which isn't out of the ordinary since I was the oldest. I remember being around seven or eight and getting upset about something. Now that I think about it, it was the demons inside me. I packed my little suitcase with some clothes and my doll and told my parents I was leaving. I walked about a mile away but went back home. I remember being a little older, and my cousin Elena, and I got caught in the barn, smoking one of my Popo's half-smoked cigarettes. I ran to the house, straight to the kitchen sink to wash my mouth out with soap. My mom asked what I was doing and why was I putting soap in my mouth. I was crying and told her we were caught smoking one of Popo's cigarettes. She hugged me and told me not to cry.

My mom sheltered us, always warning us we were going to fall or cut or hurt ourselves. Sometimes my brothers and I would get into trouble right before my daddy would get home. And there we go, having to get a spanking. When our momma would spank us, it didn't hurt near as much as when our daddy would. I wish she would have waited to tell my dad about all the things we had done wrong later in the evening instead of right when he got home. Why couldn't she wait? That way, my daddy could come home and let us run to him. It was always an exciting time when my daddy would come home. But because she would tell him about how horrible her day was first, we would get the repercussion of it.

But my father, he would cry when he spanked us. He didn't want to do it, but he knew that he needed to discipline us. Rudy and I got spanked the most. Gabriel was the smart one. He would see everything Rudy and I did wrong, and he wouldn't do it, or he just didn't get caught. Whenever we would go visit friends or family, we would get a lecture before arriving that we better act right. As a child, it felt like my parents didn't want us to be kids. I understand my parents just wanted my brothers and I to be on our best behavior. But it never failed—we would end up being told we were going to "get it" when we got home. And that meant we were going to get a spanking. I would get chills when my daddy would say that because I knew it was going to hurt. One time during one of our visits to my aunt Ruth and uncle Noe's house, I had wandered into my cousin Noe's room. I got a hold of a roll-on deodorant, thinking it was cologne. I rolled it all over my arms, my face, and my neck. When I walked out of his room and down the hallway into the living room, my aunt Ruth said, "Trudy! What do you have all over your face?" We all came to the conclusion I had put deodorant all over my body! It was so funny.

My mom and my dad got married in 1973. My daddy surrendered his life to Jesus Christ in 1974. I was born in 1976. My mom said I was her little doll when I was a little girl. She and my dad always made sure I was dressed really pretty with my hair always fixed. My grandmother Nana was a Christian and raised all her children up in the Lord. Of course, when children grow up, they have to decide what kind of life they want to live. And, well, when my parents got married, they didn't have a relationship with Jesus Christ. It wasn't until the Holy Spirit began to tug at my mom's heart that she told my dad they needed to go to church. And that is when he heard about Jesus—from a man who was sharing his testimony about the previous life he lived prior to coming to Christ. And it touched my dad's heart that he, too, wanted to experience this new life with Jesus.

I came from a Christian home. I enjoyed a lot of my childhood, but it was a strict homelife for me. As I was growing up, I was expected to talk a certain way and behave a certain way. I wasn't able to just be a kid. I remember a cousin of mine being upset with me because I had a perfect life, a perfect home, a perfect family. From the outside, yes, I can see why she would have said that. But you never really know what goes on behind closed doors. When I've talked to my brothers about certain things, they don't remember their childhood like mine. They were younger than me and didn't see the things I saw. They didn't hear or pay attention to the way things were. They weren't raised up like I was, even though we were in the same home. I didn't enjoy watching my dad give my mom the final says in our home. I didn't enjoy watching my dad not having a voice; I didn't enjoy seeing it or hearing it. I disliked my mother because of it. My father would agree with everything my mother said. It made me dislike him too.

As I was getting a little older, I felt like everything I did was never good enough—my grades, my dress style, the way I did my hair, the way I spoke, my laugh. Any and every effort I did at home or school was talked down on by my mom. Don't get me wrong—some things I did, I would get praised for. We would have great days at home, but I didn't care about that. I chose to focus on all the negativities. I had resentment, anger, frustration, and unforgiveness in my heart, and it was building up inside me and made me realize how much I hated my life. I was unhappy. I don't remember getting many hugs or kisses as a sign of love, comfort, or just because, especially as I was getting older. At that time, I didn't believe or feel that I was loved. I saw favoritism in our home through my mom with my brothers.

It made me try harder to please her, but eventually, I stopped. Our parents either mimicked the upbringing of their parents or learned a different way to raise their children. I was very unhappy and hurt about the molestation being kept a secret. I was angry and resentful to the way I was treated versus how my brothers were treated. There were no excuses for it, so I built a wall around me so they could not get close to me, so they could never hurt me again. How many of us have prayed for our parents, asking the Holy Spirit to change them, help them, and guide them in their parenting? I don't remember praying for mine that way. I remember crying out to God 'cause I was hurt. I remember crying out to Him, complaining about my situation. I received Jesus Christ into my heart at the age of five or six and was water-baptized. At the age of twelve, I was filled with the Holy Spirit at a youth conference. I was a Christian, yet I had all these thoughts, feelings, and emotions in me. I knew Satan attacked my life early. He came to kill, steal, and destroy our lives, and I was allowing him to affect mine.

Photo of Gabriel (baby brother), (Dad) Rudy, Rebecca (mom), Rudy Jr. & me

CHAPTER 2

Troubled Teen

Junior high, here I come! I was so excited to start school again. I had always loved school, the paper, the pens, wearing a backpack. I just loved learning. I was a smart kid. I usually made As and Bs. I did my best to make perfect attendance. I always received rewards in art class, English, and reading. Junior high was going to be different than elementary because we were going to have lockers, and we were going to be traveling down different hallways to get to the next class. There were going to be new students from the other elementary schools in our district. I had some classes with my friends from sixth grade, but they weren't talking to me very much. They were cheerleaders this school year, they spent so much time together during summer cheer camp, and they had a lot in common. It's always a little nerve-wracking the first day of school because you wonder if the outfit you chose was the right one. I was afraid of getting lost from one class to the next. I was in theater arts, and I really enjoyed that class. It was very easy for me to get in front of the class and speak or act. I wasn't shy when it came to theater or singing in front of people, but I was shy when it came to talking to a boy I liked. In elementary school, I liked a boy, and I told my "friend." She said she would talk to him for me, and she messed around with him instead. I couldn't believe it!

Now that I was in seventh grade, I could fit in some of my momma's clothes and heels, so I wore them to church. Man, I would get in trouble. Somehow, some way, I would always tear her pantyhose or scratch her heels. My daddy would get upset, too, because he was the one who paid for them.

My parents, my aunts from my momma's side, my cousins, and my grandmother all went to the same church—Primera Iglesia Bautista. My parents sang in the front of church. My aunts would sing. My grandmother would sing. My brothers and I would sing. My brothers and I were in all the Christmas programs and Easter plays. We were really involved in church. However, this church was a Spanish-speaking church, but my Sunday school class was taught in English. I learned how to memorize verses from the Bible and songs. During the church services, I learned how to read and write Spanish because the hymnals were in Spanish, and so were the lyrics they would put on the screen. I really loved church. I loved singing to God. All of our church family was close and felt like our real family.

Being in junior high now, I wasn't too happy about all the *No*s I would hear from my parents. No this, no that. It seemed as though the little relationship I had with my parents was falling apart. I wouldn't talk to them that much anymore. I kept everything to myself. I was really short with my answers to them. I would lie to the kids at school when they would invite me places. I would say I already had plans because I knew my parents weren't going to let me go. I wasn't allowed to listen to any music, except Christian music. I felt like I was in *prison*!

A rebellious spirit was on me. A spirit of depression and suicide, as well. I was getting in trouble at home more and more. Not like when I was a lil' kid—this was different. I would talk back to my parents and have an attitude all the time. I hated everything. If the sun was out, I hated the sun. If it was raining, I hated the rain. I was miserable. By the time I entered eighth grade, my taste for clothes had changed. I stayed to myself a lot, and I started hanging around the skaters and new wavers. I wore black and baggy pants a lot. I would wear my daddy's Levi's and my black army boots. I felt so lonely. I didn't like the way I felt inside, so I attempted my first suicide. Thank God it wasn't successful. I didn't really want to die. The school counselor called my parents. They picked me up from school and took me home. Something was wrong with me inside. I just didn't know what it was at the time. In actuality, demons were inside me, tormenting me, messing with all my emotions, and telling me to kill myself. They were the ones making me so miserable inside. They were the ones making me hate my life, hate my parents, and hate everything. Satan was trying to destroy my life before I was able to accomplish all the things God had planned for me to do. Satan will attack our lives early when we are young to destroy our future. He wants to steal our joy and peace. Satan wants to destroy our families. He wants to kill our lives. Satan hates us!

Even though I was raised in church, I didn't know God's Word and the power of the Holy Spirit. I didn't know that Satan and all his demons were under my feet. I didn't know I had the power and ability to rebuke Satan from my life. I didn't know! When we feel depressed or have thoughts of suicide or are just miserable with our lives, if we would give God an opportunity to come into our lives, He can change everything around us. God can restore your peace. He can rekindle that joy within you. God will give you the power to put Satan in his place! Satan has already been defeated, so when he tries to whisper lies to you, you can tell him to *go* because he no longer has any power over your life!

But I didn't know any of this! I didn't have the knowledge or the tools to defeat Satan and his demons! Yes, I went to church, but they didn't teach me how to cast demons from my life! They didn't warn me Satan and his demons can come in if I open a door. They didn't teach me how to use my armor. They didn't teach us! *No one taught me how to fight*! So every tactic, every trick, and every scheme Satan and his demons used on me, I fell for them.

CHAPTER 3

Most Likely to Succeed

When I started high school, there were so many kids; so many different personalities. We all had one thing in common—trying to figure out our identities. There were so many different social groups. There were the kickers, the skaters, the jocks, the preps, the heavy metals, the nerds, and the cool kids. I didn't hang around with any group in particular 'cause I got along with everyone. About five of my cousins all attended this school, so in between classes, we would meet at "The Bench," in front of the C building. I loved school. I loved to learn. I loved to read and draw. I loved music. I was young and cool. But there was something still wrong inside me. I just didn't know what it was.

I, Trudy Nunez, an A-B student, honor roll, most likely to succeed, raised in church, had both parents present, two younger brothers, and a hardworking father who taught me and loved me and a mother who showed us how to be artistic and musical, one day ran away from home. I also had run away from God's plan for my life. I ran away from my parents, my brothers, and my grandparents, who started living with us a few years before. I ran away from all my dreams and goals. What was I doing?

I don't know, but I left. It was summer of 1993, and I ran away.

My parents went looking for me and took me home and whipped me. I deserved it. I shouldn't have left. I should have stayed home, but I had so many negative emotions within me and was tired of dealing with the issues at home. I should have opened up and spoke to my parents about the things I was dealing with. I should have talked to them about the things that were troubling me, but I didn't. I should have stayed home and been obedient. I should have stayed home, finished school, graduated, and gone to college. I wanted to be a lawyer. I wanted to be an architect. I wanted to sing and draw. I was really good at it. Not realizing Satan's attack on my life, I ran, thinking it was the answer to my problems. I never knew how much I hurt my baby brother, Gabriel. We were so close. I broke his heart. He never knew what I was going through, but I never thought of the results of my actions. I was trying to escape.

The day I ran away, I met some kids. Some kids were younger than me, some were older, and some my age. They were all running the streets, coming and going as they pleased. Not one parent telling these kids what to do. Not one parent ordering these kids around. They had no rules, seemed like! They were smoking cigarettes and cussing. I thought, *Wow! Compared to my life, these kids are free*, and I was in prison. Boy, did I want to be like them.

Little did I know how my life would turn out. That moment right there was the choice of what path I would lead. That decision changed my whole life.

Why couldn't I just go back home? Why did I run away and stop going to school? Why didn't I just go home? Because I hated my life at home. I hated being home. I hated how I felt when I was home. I lost nineteen years of my life because of the road I chose. And I would like to encourage you—not to run but to learn to face whatever is before you, to listen to your parents and talk to them, to work it out, to let them know how you feel, and to find a church where they teach from the Bible. A church where you can see self-growth. I want to encourage you to love your family, honor your parents, and pursue your goals, no matter what. We have a Father who loves us. He loves you very much and has a perfect plan for your life. I don't know what kind of situation you are in right now, but it is not the end. If you will turn to God and seek Him with all of your heart, He can turn your whole life around. God can restore your life back and give you more. He wants to give you true peace in your life.

He wants to let you know how much He loves you. He loves you so much that He gave His Son, Jesus, to die on the cross for your sins so that you could live free and, one day, live with Him in heaven. I want you to know that, once you surrender your life to God, He will perfect everything that concerns you. Every blessing and promise in the Bible will belong to you. We go through life trying to do things our way, but our way is never the right way. And we will continue to go in circles until we allow Him in our life. Until we receive the truth of who we are and the power God has given us, by giving us the Holy Spirit, we will always be victims to Satan and his demons attacking our lives. Until we have the knowledge and tools of how to defeat every assignment Satan has to destroy our lives, we will always be his punching bag. But it is time for us to fight back! And the only way to fight back is to ask God to come into your heart. Ask God to forgive you of all your sins, and ask the Holy Spirit to come in. Once you do that, God gives you the power to cast out demons from your life! You call each demon by name and cast them out in the name of Jesus and send them to the abyss! The abyss is a black hole where they can *never* return to torment anyone again. You see, once you are saved, you are a child of God. And He has seated you together with Him in heavenly places (a place of authority) above any evil spirit, evil powers, and principalities. He places everything under your feet! So Satan, his demons, and his assignments against you and your family no longer have any power over you. God has set you free! However, you must cast any demons from your life who have been hiding within you. Call them out by name! Demon of depression, I cast you out in the name of Jesus and throw you into the abyss! Demon of cancer, I rebuke you in the name of Jesus and throw you into the abyss! Demon of anxiety, demon of suicide, demon of autism, demon of confusion, demon of manipulation, demon of anger, demon of murder, demon of lying, and demon of stress—call them out by name! Cast them out in the name of Jesus and throw them into the abyss! You have to be born again. "Born again" means you have surrendered your life to God and made Him the Lord of your life. If you aren't born again and you cast out demons from your life, they will come back and bring seven more demons because you don't have Jesus in your heart, nor do you have the Holy Spirit inside. So be sure to have given your life to Jesus as I said above. Look, I want you set free from the chains Satan has had you bound with. And God wants you set free as well! He came to set the captives free. I was held captive! But no one helped me or showed me how to get the chains of Satan off of me.

CHAPTER 4

I Was Addicted

What a cold winter 1993 was. I would sleep on porches; I would sleep at the barrio park. I would sleep outside because I would rather be out there on the streets than at my home. Sometimes I would sneak into one of the homeboy's houses and shower when their parents would leave in the morning for work. What was I thinking? I had my own room at home, a warm house with parents who love me. I do believe my parents loved me, but at the time, I didn't. I was believing the lies of the devil. I refused to go back home because I was so stubborn and hardheaded. I would rather go through all of that than surrender to my parents.

After running away three times, my parents finally decided to just let me go. I was going to have to learn the hard way. My momma would make her way to go look for me out in the streets. She would give me twenty dollars here and there so I could have some money in my pocket. I remember my parents brought me a Dallas Cowboy jacket for Christmas so I could be warm. They would ask me if I would like to go home, but I was having too much fun being free. I had begun to smoke cigarettes and drink alcohol. Every now and then a few homeboys would huff spray paint from a brown paper bag, so I tried it. I didn't like that too much. The homeboys all had a tattoo somewhere on their body, and I wanted one too! They told me I had to get jumped in the gang before I could get a dog tattoo. So, there I go, I had to fight Big G, Diablo, Chuya and another homeboy. Next thing I know, I'm a barrio dog! I had these steel-toe boots that I wore. And I was walking down the street and Brotha Man saw me and called me Troop and so that name stuck.

I hadn't been away from home long, and I was already getting introduced to cocaine. I had never seen it before; I had never seen drugs or done drugs before. And here I was living a life totally opposite of who I was raised to become. Never in my life could I have imagined all the things that were to come. So the homeboys were talking about shooting up the cocaine with a needle. I wanted to try it! Diablo told me no because I was going to like it too much, but he gave it to me anyway. And he was right, I did like it! When I would get a little money from my mom, I would buy a twenty of coke. But because I didn't know too much about it, they would always dilute mine with water. So I learned how to fix the needle and dope myself. I got so good; they would jokingly call me nurse. Due to my innocent face, they would have me go into the pharmacy to grab a bag of needles. A little taste here, a little taste there, man, I wanted to do it all the time.

I was *addicted*! Being addicted to drugs with no job and no money, you have to come up with ways to get money. And so, you steal, you lie, you rob, and you do things you don't want to do. You are doing things you thought you would never do. Being addicted to drugs causes your appearance to change; it causes you to lose weight. Being addicted to drugs makes you put everything that is the most important on the last place. Being addicted to drugs or alcohol causes you to lose everything. Drugs are not prejudice. They don't care who you are. Drugs don't care about what family you come from. Drugs will fool you. They make you think you can control it, but it will destroy your life. If you have never done drugs, praise God! If you have done drugs, then you know what I am talking about.

Being around all my homeboys, living on the streets, was what I wanted. They all accepted me for who I was. I didn't have to pretend to be anybody else. They were my new family. They were all looking out for me, making sure I had somewhere to stay and making sure I had something to eat.

There were a few times when some of my family came to save me. Tia Hopie went and picked me up and took me to live with her in Houston. I know she loved me and was trying to get me into a new environment. I stayed with her for a little while but wanted to go back. It was the drugs I was missing. I was addicted to coke. And I wasn't ready to stop. Aunt Ruth and Uncle Noe took me in at a different time. It was one of the times I got out of jail. So I was doing good for a little bit. They trusted me and let me go and come as I pleased. But I ended up back on the streets. Just because I would go to jail and get clean for a little while, I and everyone else thought I was good. But if we never truly allow God to change our lives or until we are truly ready to change, it will never happen.

CHAPTER 5

You Think You Know What Love Is

My life on the streets consisted of me bouncing from house to house. None of them disrespected me. We all got along really well. And during this time, Diablo and I were starting to like each other. We would mess around, and we'd get high together. If he got a twenty of coke, he would share with me. If I got some, I would share with him. I ended up moving in with him early that year in 1994. Of course, because I was living with him, I gave myself to him. I knew I was doing something wrong because I was raised to wait until you get married, but I did it anyway. And I cried—cried because I knew I shouldn't have. We got along really great especially when drugs were involved. We would get ready in the morning and stay gone all day. We would come home, and his cousin would cook dinner for us. She was always so nice. The house was full—his mom, his grandmother, his brother, his uncle, his cousins, and me—but we all got along really well.

I know that Diablo's previous relationships were not too good. I had heard that he would cheat on them and beat them up. I don't know why that wasn't a reg flag for me. I started to notice a change in his behavior. He had started to talk to me differently; he had started to treat me differently. He would tell me that I had to stay home, and he was leaving. I was like "what?" I'm not staying home. And then we would argue and fight. That was the whole reason I ran away from home—because I didn't want anybody telling me what I could and couldn't do.

He started to abuse me. He would call me all these horrible names and say horrible things to me. He crushed my self-esteem. He was breaking me emotionally. He would be so mean to me and would try to keep me away from everyone. The few times I would come outside, he would belittle me in front of the homeboys. It was so embarrassing.

Why didn't I go home then? Why did I think I deserved that? Why did I think I had to stay with someone who treated me this way? Why did I think it was okay to be treated this way? Why didn't I say "NO MORE"? I DESERVE BETTER! I DESERVE TO BE LOVED. I DESERVE TO BE WITH SOMEONE WHO LOVES ME!

It was May 1994 when I found out I was pregnant. And once I knew this precious baby was inside of me, I quit doing drugs; I quit smoking and drinking. Why did I stay? I had a home to go to. I had a family who loved me. Why was I at a place and with someone who didn't love me back? Why was I letting someone disrespect me? Why didn't I leave? When my parents would drive through the barrio to see me, they could see the bruises on me. I would lie. I would tell them that I had fallen or hit myself on something. I know that they knew the truth.

I continued to let him mistreat me. I stayed because I loved him. He would walk out of the door and jump in the car of another woman, and I would welcome him home as though he did nothing.

CHAPTER 6

Just Wanted to Be Loved

I had to leave! I wasn't going to continue to live there with him like that. I decided to go live with my parents, where my baby and I could be safe. I was going to name her Odessa Rhea. She saved my life. I was on a road to death because of the drugs I was using and the way I was using them. If it wasn't for her being conceived in my belly, I wouldn't have stop doing drugs. I liked them too much. I believe this was one of God's attempts to save me from myself.

Of course, I was hurt because of all the cheating, all the lying, all the abuse, all the arguments, and all the hurtful words that can't be taken back. I loved him, and I wanted it to work; but he didn't want to stop using, and the way he was treating me wasn't getting any better. *Why didn't he love me?* I thought. Why did he hurt me like this? Why did I think this unhealthy relationship was normal? I knew he loved me, but he was on drugs. And he didn't have any male role models to follow as in a healthy relationship. We were both young. We were both lost. I am not making excuses for him, but hurt people hurt people. He had so much happened to him, too, as a child—had no father, only a single mother. He was raised by his grandmother and his mom. No one in his family were Christians, so there was no one teaching him anything about God. Then again, I was raised in church, and look how my life had turned out.

Domestic violence is not okay. Physical, mental, and emotional abuse are all the same. We do not deserve it! And we shouldn't keep taking them back just because they say sorry. If a person is truly sorry, they will change. I know sometimes we are too scared to leave the abuser. We think no one else will love us or accept us. We sometimes think we wouldn't be able to survive financially without them. We can't imagine our life without the abuser. The abuser knocks us down so much that we lose our confidence, and we become insecure. The abuser will tear us down as much as they can, as much as we let them.

Now that I had moved back into my parents' house, I was on a road to rebuild my life. The remainder of my pregnancy was awesome. My dad and my mom would help me, and if I was craving a certain food, my dad would make sure to get it for me. My dad would bring me a whopper home from Burger King every day. I was home, and my parents were helping me get all the things I would need for my new baby. We got her a crib and some clothes; everything was good. I was going back to church. I received my GED and enrolled into college. I was taking my basics and wanted to major in psychology. I really loved going to school. I loved learning, and I loved knowing that I was on a new path with a brighter future for my daughter and myself.

When Odessa arrived, she brought so much joy into the home. She had such a personality, and she loved taking pictures. My brothers were still living at home, so she had all of us to love her. She was very smart; she absorbed everything like a sponge. She knew colors, numbers, and the alphabet before the age of two and enjoyed having conversations as though she was an adult.

After a few months, I decided to get a part-time job. I inquired in signing up for the Marine Corps but would not qualify because I was a single mother. So I enrolled back into college.

CHAPTER 7

Things Are Looking Up

The phone rang; it was Diablo. He said that he had changed. He said he was working now and stopped doing drugs. So Odessa and I moved back in with him. Everything was going well for a little while. One thing I know, if he wanted to use drugs or drink, I didn't say *no* strong enough. So we would do it. And if I wanted to do drugs or drink, his *no* wasn't strong enough either.

It breaks my heart, thinking of what I exposed Odessa to. One moment she is my world. I protected her, I took care of her, I taught her, and I loved her. And the next moment, I'm back in an unhealthy relationship. All of the abusive behavior toward me was over; we just had a drug problem. And we were very unhealthy for each other. I remember Odessa knocking on the bathroom door, calling me. She wanted me; she was asking what I was doing. But her dad and I were shooting up. I'd have to tell her we would be out in a minute. He would work all week just for us to spend his whole check before Monday.

My daughter, I love you so much! Why did I do this to you? Why did I do this to myself? I hate that drugs stole that time from me. I hate that drugs robbed you of time with me.

This wasn't the last time I went back with him. It was a pattern between me and him. We would get back with each other for a little while, and then I'd leave. When I would go back to live with my parents, it would hurt them every time I left. Of course, they didn't want me to get hurt again, and I don't even know if they knew we were doing drugs together. And of course, me taking my baby girl back and forth wasn't good either.

After five years of this cycle, we finally got our life together. We got married. We were going to church. We were the leaders of the youth group. We were serving the Lord, life was good! We were pregnant with Vinessa. Oh, what a big baby I was having. My belly was much bigger than it was when I was pregnant with Odessa. We were so happy! Our little family was growing. There were no drugs in our life, no alcohol. Our precious little baby brought so much joy to our lives. And our marriage was great.

We had moved into the church house. They said if we remodeled it, we could live in it, with rent, of course. We painted it. We put in new light fixtures and installed new carpet. It was our new home. Oh, I finally had everything I had hoped for—my husband, my daughters, and a new little puppy. Odessa and Vinessa had their own room. It was great! Vinessa was such a beautiful little baby girl. She looked like a porcelain doll. Such beautiful hazel eyes and golden-brown hair. We were definitely blessed with two beautiful very smart babies.

The church had told us that a new pastor would be coming to lead the church and would be needing to live in the church home together with his family. We were devastated. We felt betrayed and lied to. We were told we could live there if we remodeled the home, and now we have to pack up our family and find somewhere to live. How could they do this to us?

We found an apartment available all the way in Dickinson. And instead of trusting the Lord, instead of continuing our walk with the Lord, we walked away from God and from the church. We were so hurt. And when a person doesn't learn a new healthy way to respond to problems, they go back to what they have always done. So for us, that was drugs and alcohol. Here we go again, opening the door to drugs and alcohol in our home, in my life, and in my children's lives.

True, we weren't doing drugs and alcohol every day or even every weekend, but they were in our lives. Why didn't we or I just ask God to help me forgive them for what the church had done to us and ask God to heal our hurt? Why did I completely quit? Why did I completely turn away from God?

Why can't I get this life right? How much longer will I destroy my life? When will I be able to hold my head up high and be proud of all I'm doing? When will my children be proud of me?

When we are rooted in the Lord, when we are grounded in Him, we are not easily moved. When our foundation is built on Him and we are reading the Word daily, we are made strong so that when storms and challenges come our way, we are not shaken. We don't quit, and we don't quit walking with the Lord. Life brings trials, storms, difficulties. Problems are not prejudice. They come to everyone. The key is how you respond to the situations that come. How do you respond?

God's Word is made available to us as a manual. In the Word, we will find our purpose in life. In the Bible, we will find out who God is and who we really are. The Word of God is a mirror, and as we look into that mirror, it is so important not to forget what the mirror says about ourselves. The enemy wants to throw whatever he can at us to get us off God's perfect plan. We are so special. We carry something so special that the enemy is trying to destroy. Satan is trying to steal the crown of glory from your head. Satan and his demons never sleep. They work 24-7. They lie waiting for opportunities to distract, to tempt, to suggest, and to whisper to you to destroy your life. And if we aren't daily putting on the armor of God and if we don't know we have the power to rebuke them, they will continually get over on you. God has called you to be an overcomer! He has called you to reign in this life. Overcoming Satan and any obstacle he brings your way! You don't have to fall victim to his attacks; you just have to follow God. Allow God to lead you and guide you. Read His Word and apply it to your life. You will begin to see a transformation working inside you!

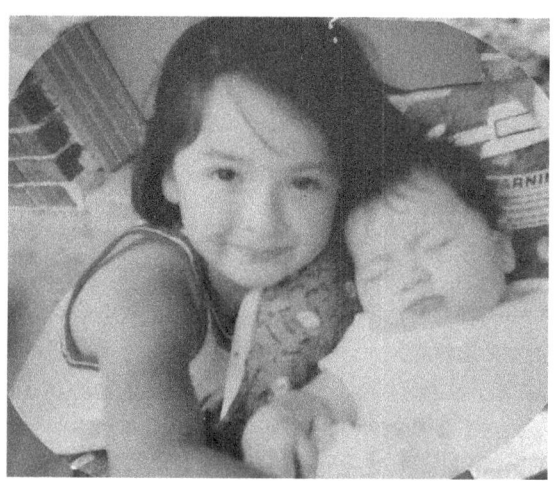

Odessa & Vinessa 2000

CHAPTER 8

Our Choices Have Consequences

We had moved to Clear Lake and started over in a new place. We were doing good. Diablo was working, and I was a full-time momma. Every now and then, I would get a little job here and there. But I really didn't have to work. My grandfather Ricardo was ill and soon after passed away. This broke me. I went into a deep depression. I couldn't get out of bed because I just couldn't. I didn't want to. I was so hurt inside. And I didn't have the Lord in my life, so I didn't even think to call on Him.

You see, all I would have had to do was call out to my God. He hears us and answers us. He is the answer. Jesus Christ is the Prince of Peace, and that's exactly what I needed—peace. I needed God. I needed my heavenly Father. I was lost. One day, one of my cousins invited me out. She said I needed to get out. So I went with her. We ended up going to a local bar in Alvin. In my mind, I had a good time. I was drinking, listening to music, and playing pool. One time turned into every weekend for a few weeks. And that was it. I was back doing drugs and drinking.

Diablo and I separated. We let the apartment go. He went back to his mother's and I went to live with my parents. I had started selling dope—I was good at it. I wasn't happy with the decisions I was making. I wanted to get back with Diablo, but it was too late; he had moved on. One weekend, Diablo was going to be picking up the girls, so I sent a letter to him in Vinessa's backpack. Vinessa told me that the lady Diablo was seeing threw it away. So it never got to him.

My daughters and I were hurt. Our little family would not be getting back together. When storms came my way, I had taught myself to run. I had trained myself to run to drugs and alcohol. But the only thing now is—I am not alone. I had my daughters. We were living with my parents, and one day, I left. I left my daughters to be raised by my mom and my dad. I left them to be brought up the exact way I was, and I hated that. But there was no way I could take them with me. There was no way I was going to let them see me living the way I lived when I would go to the streets. I wanted better for them. But better would have been me raising them, providing for them, teaching them, and loving them. But not only are my babies facing "I no longer have my daddy" but now also "I don't have my mommy either."

I was wrong. I should have grabbed ahold of my daughters and hugged them. I should have kissed their little faces and told them that everything was going to be okay. I should have told them that we were going to make it! I should have turned to God for help. I should have asked the Holy Spirit to guide me and lead me. Instead, I ran away. I was angry inside! I had so much unforgiveness in my heart.

Why didn't I think more clearly? Why didn't I stop and think first?

It is so important to allow God to heal us from the inside out. It is vital for Him to come in and make us complete. This world is full of disappointments. There are people who will let us down, and it hurts. We must have a healthy way of getting through the situation. When we receive Jesus Christ into our hearts and make Him our Lord, the old person and our old ways are dead. The old way of doing things, the old way of speaking, the old way of thinking—it has all disappeared. We are now a new creation; we are now born of God. And when we are born of God, the Bible says that "we overcome the world." We have the ability to overcome every obstacle that comes our way. We don't have to allow every little thing bother us, affect us, or discourage us. Greater is He that is in us than he that is in the world. If I had known God's truth, my life would have turned out so different. The Bible says the old has passed away and all things become new. Your outside body looks the same, but it is your spirit on the inside that is different. You are a spirit just like God is a spirit. You live in a body, so you are able to live and function on this earth. And you have a soul. Your soul is where your emotions, thoughts, and will come from. But the real you is your spirit. You have to retrain yourself. You were raised a certain way and learned different characteristics from many people and picked up all kinds of habits. You learned behaviors and learned how to act or react when certain things come your way. You are a reflection of Him once you are born again. But if a person isn't taught the Word correctly, then they suffer as I did.

Me & my daughters Odessa & Vinessa 2004

CHAPTER 9

Why Can't I Get It Right?

My daughters Odessa and Vinessa are now twenty-six and twenty-one. They themselves are mommas now. I thank God every day that I have my daughters in my life. I thank God for my grandbabies; they are so precious to me. I praise God! He allows me the opportunity to minister to them, give them godly advice, and pray over them. The day I walked out of prison in December 2009, I let them know immediately that I had already served my time for all that I had done. I told them that God had already forgiven me for all I did. And that they were not going to rub in my face my past. That person was long gone. I told them that I am their momma, and they were going to respect me.

I hurt both of my daughters for so many years. I was lost. My parents took on the role of their parents. In my mind, while I was out selling dope, I thought I was being a good momma because I would bring home a bag of new clothes or toys. I would give my parents money for food or just because I knew they were watching them. Every time I would come home, the visits were always cut short. Either my phone was going off for someone who needed dope, or I needed to go get a hit for myself.

I thought I was a good mom. I was so blind! I would think that those material things would make up for my absence. It was my way of showing them I love them. I know they would much rather have me than any of those things. A lot of responsibilities fell on Odessa.

She didn't ask for this. But this little child has been thrown into a position to look after Vinessa. She was her big sister. They always slept together and shared the same room. They had a special relationship; they kept each other happy. They made up funny jokes, and they kept themselves busy while I was away, whether on the streets or in jail/prison. I regret not being there for the times Odessa was getting bullied in junior high. I regret not being there for either of them. It still crushes me today. And I know that God has forgiven me, but it still hurts my heart.

It took me a very long time to finally forgive myself for putting my children through this.

Why, Trudy? Why couldn't you open your eyes? Why wouldn't you just stop?

My daughters would cry as I would walk out the door, but the drugs, the addiction, and the money were so much stronger. It would hurt me as I would leave. My daughters are my life! I wanted to protect them from seeing what I was doing or what I had become.

I used to be such a wonderful momma, taking care of my baby girls. Living for my babies. Living a good clean life. But if conflict came, I didn't know how to handle it. I had already programmed myself to run to drugs and alcohol.

Why? Why didn't I run to Jesus? I never meant to hurt my girls. I thought I was only hurting myself. But I was hurting my children. I was hurting my parents, my brothers, and my grandma.

While I was out there on the streets, it made it easier for me to use dope because I'm thinking about how I can just leave my babies. So I would use to forget. I would use to forget all the tragedies in my life. I would use to drown all the pain I had inside. I would use to forget all the hurt people caused me. Once that high was gone, reality hits, and then I have to use again to drown it all away.

It's just a cycle that goes on over and over again. And you think that you have it under control, but you don't! You begin to lose everything, even yourself. You see, drugs don't solve the problems. They only make the problems worse. Drugs may temporarily take them away, but nothing heals you for real. It is a mirage. It's a lie from the enemy. I was drowning, and I didn't know how to get out! I wanted to change, but I didn't know how. There were times I would get out of jail and be good. I would be home with them, but I would get disappointed because either no one would give me a job or I would get into an argument with my mom. And then back to the streets I would go.

Me & my daughters Odessa & Vinessa

CHAPTER 10

What a Disappointment

My visits with my daughters were short. My visits were always unexpected. I would just pop in at any moment. They really never knew when I would show up. I had a cell phone, so I would call my mom from time to time. I would like to say every day, but I doubt it. My parents never kept my daughters from me, except for the times I tried to take them with me. It would end in yelling and screaming and fighting. I wanted my daughters, but I wasn't in a good state of living to take them. How could I raise my children being addicted to drugs? I know that they would take my girls to different places and buy them toys or gifts to get their minds off of their mom being gone. I know that they did their very best to raise them.

I'd come home, maybe eat sometimes, maybe help them with a bubble bath. I would speed-read a book to them while they played in the tub. Why? 'Cause I needed another hit! I was controlled by it! I was a slave to it! We would make a fort and play a little while. I would come home for bedtime, but I'd be gone by the time they woke up in the morning.

Trudy! You are such a disappointment!

I'm such a disappointment to myself! And because I know this and because I know that drugs have taken control of my life, I am so ashamed of who I have become—so I use! Being on the streets isn't always a pretty sight. I wouldn't sleep for days; the longest was twenty-one days. I wouldn't eat. I wouldn't shower. I would go into random convenient stores and use their restroom to freshen up if I could. I usually carried a bag or backpack with me everywhere I went. It carried my clothes, shoes, makeup, perfume, toothbrush, toothpaste, hairbrush, shampoo, and soap.

Sometimes my visits home were to finally get some sleep and eat and take a lovely hot shower. My mom has had to take off my clothes, get me in the tub, take me a bath, get me out of the tub, get me dressed, and put me to bed. I would get all the rest I needed, usually three days. I would wake up and eat, spend a little time with Odessa and Vinessa, then go back to bed. Once I was rested up, I would leave again.

When will my eyes open? When will I realize how precious this time is? I was blinded to the truth. I couldn't see what was really going on. When will I live a life with purpose?

I sold drugs, yes, I was addicted to the power behind it. The thrill of everyone needing you. But they don't need you! They need the drugs that you have! But once you taste the dope for yourself, then your supply is to make profit, to buy more, and to support your own habit. Every time I would get locked up, I would lose everything—all my clothes, CDs, phone, shoes, perfumes. Whatever I had were gone. So every time I got out, I would have to rebuild my empire. It is a hard game to get out of.

It isn't easy facing the truth. It isn't easy admitting all of your faults. It's hard to say "I messed up and I am sorry." I am guilty of everything that I did. I hurt my children! I abandoned my daughters. I chose dope over my babies. I allowed all the disappointments in my life to cause myself to not only hurt myself but hurt the little innocent girls who love me to death! I cannot change yesterday. I can't change it! I wish I could. I would take my time; I would take my time with my little baby girls. I would take my time and brush their hair. I would lie with them and read them a book before bed. I would go outside and run and play. But I can't fix what I did in the past!

IT'S NEVER TOO LATE

Odessa, Vinessa & Trudy 2005

CHAPTER 11

Too Pretty to Use Drugs

During 1997 until 1998, in between one of the breakups with Diablo, I had gotten really close to one of my homeboys Chuya. I didn't really have anyone else to speak to about what I was going through with Diablo. I surely couldn't speak to his family nor mine. And so, I would talk to Chuya. He was a little younger than me, but I caught feelings for him and him for me. We would talk. We would laugh. We got along really well. He never really liked the fact that I was doing drugs. He hated that I would shoot up. He would say I was "too pretty for that." He would tell me that I was too good for that. One day, he just said he wanted me to quit. But, of course, I couldn't; I didn't want to! And so, we stopped seeing each other. He went his way, and I went mine. If we ever saw each other at a party or wherever, we would still act like we were together. But eventually, he moved on.

I wasn't going to stop doing drugs, and I wasn't going to let anyone tell me I had to. In my mind, I felt like I had run away from rules when I left my parent's house, so I didn't want anyone telling me what I could and couldn't do. In actuality, being such a young girl and being sexually abused, there was a sense of no control. And then, when I finally told my parents about it, they did nothing; and so a feeling of no self-worth, I wanted that control. I wanted to be able to say what I wanted, do what I wanted, be who I wanted.

I felt as though I was not enough to defend. I wasn't worth protecting. I felt unloved. I had resentment in my heart for so many years. I had unforgiveness in my heart and hate. I never felt like anything I did was good enough. All my effort, all my talent, all my good grades—everything and anything I ever did was never good enough. I remember all throughout my life as a teen or out on the streets, I would relate everything—my actions, my situations, and my storms—to movies like *The Rose* or *The Doors*. I would hear or sing songs that would ease me throughout my journey, whether walking the streets or sleeping outside or being lost in the streets of Houston, addicted to dope. Some songs helped me, and some made me feel even worse. I felt at times that my life was a movie, waiting for the happy ending, but it seemed to never come.

I was unhappy growing up. And when I was lost out in the streets, everything my mom would tell me would just push me away further. She said she would say things in a manner that maybe I would open my eyes, but it just made me resent her more. And when I got with Diablo, whom I lost my virginity to, and he told me that he loved me, just to only hit me and cheat on me, it messed me up inside, in my mind and in my heart. Did I deserve this? No! Of course not! Was I too good for this? Using drugs? Being on the street? If only I had reached out to God, Abba, my Father! I never asked Him to heal my broken heart. I never asked Him to cleanse my heart from all the pain and anger. I never asked Him to save me from myself.

In the midst of every mistake, my heavenly Father was right there waiting for me all along. He was waiting and watching me, He was protecting me. I went through hell because of all of *my* choices. I put myself through horrible things. But my God had a different plan for my life.

Chuya (Jesus) & Trudy 1994

CHAPTER 12

Why Didn't You Just Go Home?

I have been raped four times from 2001 to 2007 by different men. Being raped did harm me on the inside mentally, physically, emotionally, and spiritually. It was painful. They hurt me! It was so scary because I never knew what the rapist was thinking. I didn't know what their intentions were. Were they going to get off of me and leave, or were they going to kill me? Or maybe they saw me around the neighborhood smoking dope and just thought they could take advantage of a young girl who didn't belong there. After the first rape, I felt like trash, like a disgrace. I felt so dirty and ashamed. It takes a brave victim to speak up, but I never did. I was raped! I was taken advantage of not just once! How could someone do this to me! And why? I know their faces. I would constantly see their faces in my mind. I felt like I put myself in those places for something like that to happen to me. I let people hurt me. Was I that damaged to believe it was okay? Had I been beaten down so much in my spirit that I thought it was okay for all these things to happen to me? After the first two times, I stopped fighting back and only hoped they would let me go and live. I had put myself in situations like these for this to happen to me. I would be at different crack houses, either smoking there or waiting for a dealer to show up. If I had enough money, I would rent a hotel for the night. I didn't deserve this! I didn't deserve to be raped. Some of these rapists, I knew. One man raped me while my husband Diablo was passed out drunk in the other room. I never told him. I never told anyone. My hate for men was growing. When I was in Houston, I was selling dope in a neighborhood I shouldn't have been in; and so this guy jumped out of the car with three other guys, putting a gun to my head, telling me to leave. Thank God he didn't shoot me.

I have had a gun to my face two different times. One of these times was because I was in the wrong neighborhood, trying to sell dope. One day I was walking down the street, and a guy I knew from one of the crack houses was driving by. He had a girl in the front seat and a guy in the back seat and asked if I needed a ride. I said sure. I had just scored, so my pockets were full of money and dope. Well, I found out the three of them had been partying for the past three days and ran out of dope so left their hotel. Just my luck, the driver starts tripping out, saying that I owed him something since he gave me dope the past three days. I told him he had the wrong person. He stopped at the gas station on Cullen to put gas. He starts yelling at me that I better give him something or he was going to tax me, which I had no idea what that meant. I kept telling him that he didn't party with me, and I wasn't going to give him any of my dope. He swings at my head right at the temple. I didn't realize what had happened but felt something warm dripping down my face and hands. I looked, and it was blood! I jumped out of his ride and ran into the store, looking for someone to call for help, but no one wanted to help me. I ran to the restroom to see what happened to me. My jaw was hanging from my face. I tried to clean myself the best I could. My cousin used to live close by that area, and I took off to his house. I knocked on his door and asked him for a gun. I told him that someone had broken my jaw and I wanted a gun. He didn't want to give me a gun and told me to be careful. I didn't want to stay at his house. Stubborn me wanted to go back to the street to score and get high. I've been in many dangerous situations. I have been beaten many times by different men. They would stomp on my head and my body until I wouldn't move anymore. I have been homeless. I have been hungry and lost. I have been broken. I have been abused sexually, mentally, and emotionally. I have been a drug addict and alcoholic.

I remember crying walking down the streets of Houston or Alvin or wherever I was, asking God to please save me! I carried a journal around with me. I would write all my pain each day of the journey. I was so miserable. I was so lost. I was so hurt.

I have been arrested more than twenty-six times. Twenty-six times, dang it! I guess I just wasn't ready to change. I wanted a different life, but I guess I just wasn't tired of it.

Year after year, every year, two to three times a year, I was in Brazoria County Jail. I lived there! It was like my second home. The streets and the jail raised me. I was watching my daughters grow up from behind a glass window. I was hurting me and I was hurting them!

Odessa and Vinessa would pray for me every day. They were fighting for me in the spiritual realm! They were fighting for their momma. They loved me so much. Their love for me was true love. They loved me no matter what. No matter what I had done, they loved me. Their love kept me alive! It kept me going. Their love gave me a reason to live!

There were many times that I had tried to kill myself. I was just so miserable. I wanted to be with my babies, but I couldn't. I wanted a different life, but no matter what, I just couldn't get it. I just couldn't get it right. I didn't know how to.

The tracks on my arm were hideous. I would wear sports bands of assorted colors to match my outfit to disguise these hideous scars, some old, some fresh. Poke, poke, poke until all my veins collapsed, and I couldn't hit anymore. I would shoot in my arms, hands, legs, and feet when I couldn't shoot anywhere else. When you are craving that hit, you keep stabbing yourself until you find a vein that works. I've poked myself so much I busted the vein, with blood coming out of my mouth from the damage to my arm.

OD'ing in front of my cousin once scared him. He told me I could never shoot up in front of him again. He said he wouldn't want to be the one to tell my parents I had died. I died in front of two other cousins once in his trailer. I saw them both shaking my body. I was floating above them, watching them.

I remember fixing up a needle so strong with dope ready to kill myself at my Popo's grave. Crazy, right? I realized I didn't want my daughters to wake up the next day with the news that they found their momma dead at the cemetery. I didn't want them to be the laughingstock at school, especially when the kids already said stuff to them about me.

Trudy, why didn't you just stay home and listen to your parents? Why didn't you want to follow their rules? I wish I could hug you and tell you that I love you and I am so sorry that you went through all of this.

There was one particular police officer in Alvin named Officer Edwards who, whenever he got me handcuffed in his car, would ask me when I was going to do something better with my life. He would ask me when I was going to get off the streets and make something of myself. I am so thankful to him. He may not realize it, but he was planting seeds into my spirit. He was being the voice of the Lord, showing love to me just by saying those simple words.

Every time I'd get locked up, I'd write letters back home, saying that this time was going to be different when I get out. The first few times I would get released, everyone, even me, thought I was going to do good. We all thought just because I sat in jail for a little while and got off the dope, that I was going to do great. After a while, everyone's expectations of me changing was low. You could bet on me messing up again. I would tell the guards at Brazoria County, "I'll be back. Save me a bunk." I would make remarks like "you should write my name on my bunk and reserve it for me." And sure enough, I was back doing all I knew: selling and doing drugs. I would stay clean for a little while, but if my mom and I would bump heads or she would say something wrong, I would take off. Why? Sooner or later, no one expected me to get better. They would hope, but I would always let them down. But you could count on me messing up again. It was expected of me to not do good for very long. It had to be a move of God to change my life. It had to be God, and it had to be me finally tired of living without Him.

But there I go again, messing up my life. And once I'm out there, the guilt kicks in. Of how I always mess up. Of how I always disappointed my family. Of how I abandoned my children. I would replay all the arguments and every mistake, all the shame and guilt I had caused my family. It would always be an excuse to use. And once I'm using, I have to start selling so I can support my habit.

I have had twenty-one overdoses! Some of these overdoses were by accident, but most of them were on purpose. I wanted to end my pain! I wanted to end my baby girl's pain! I thought death was my answer. I was listening to all the lies of Satan that everyone would be better off without me! I was so disappointed in myself! I was so tired of all of it! I wanted to end it all! I was so tired of hurting my babies.

I always saw myself as a strong person—a problem-solver. I had a strong will, always challenged when someone said I couldn't do something. I never saw myself as a quitter. I always considered myself as a leader. Every hurt, every bad decision, every disappointment, every tear I caused my daughters, every reason why tears came from me made my heart so hard. Because I sold dope, I could load up my pipe with however much I wanted. I made me "master blasters" all the time. I'd later sell my pipe for money because it was loaded with so much resin.

The enemy puts lies in our heads that our lives are over, that we could never get our children back. He tries to fill our minds with lies to get us to quit. It is like a battle. He throws a jab at us, waiting to see if we will bite the bait. He keeps throwing jabs at us until we finally just want to end it all. He wants us depressed, feeling lonely, suicidal, heartbroken, and angry. He tells us everything opposite of what God's Word says about us. We need to open up the Bible, ask the Holy Spirit to give us understanding of what we are reading, and let His Word get planted into our spirit. His Word is a mirror of who we were are. The Bible is a mirror of who He created us to be and who He really is. There is so much more to being a believer than accepting Jesus into our hearts and then one day going to heaven. God intended His children to live victoriously in this life! We are a reflection of our Father. We are witnesses that He is real. As we grow in the knowledge of His Word, we are able to enjoy all the benefits He has for us! If we never know what inheritance He left us, how can we bask in them? If you are going through a tough time right now, I want you to go wash your face. God created you for something great!

He has a perfect plan for your life. As you seek Him, He will add to your life.

As you hear more about Him, your faith will grow. You will begin to see God moving and working in your life. You will be on the right path. You will be at the right place at the right time because He leads you. Don't forget all that God has done in the past. Remember all the times He has saved you. Remember all the times He made a way for you when there was no way. Don't forget how He saved you, protected you. When you are on God's path and you know that He is leading you and time after time He has delivered you, why would you worry now? Satan wants you worried and afraid. But we, as the children of God, don't live by our sensory perception. We live by every word that comes out of the mouth of God. We don't fear. We don't respond the way a nonbeliever would.

God says, "I will do exceedingly abundantly above all you could ever ask or think according to the power in you!" God's children have power to change any situation! Believers have the power to cause God to do the impossible. How? By the power in you! You have to open your mouth and speak what God's Word says. Don't give room to the enemy to lie to you. Say "I disarm you spirit of fear!" I will overcome every situation that comes my way because greater is He that is in me than he that is in the world. I never fail. I never lose because God is with me! He will deliver me because He loves me. I am an heir to the throne. I am born of God, not of man. Everything I touch prospers in the name of Jesus. My God is with me! Not only is He with me, He lives inside me! Hallelujah!

CHAPTER 13

They Couldn't Depend on Me

December 2007, the judge told me, "Trudy, I am tired of seeing you in my courtroom. If I see you in my courtroom one more time, I am giving you ten years in prison." I said, "Yes, sir." I got out and went back to the street. I had come up with a plan and my goal was to be home with my daughters. So January 2008, I had three drug houses. I distributed my phones to three workers. I was never going to have to sell on the streets again, so I thought. I was going to let my workers do all the street work, and I just drop off the products. I was going to be a boss. I was finally going to be home and be the mother my children needed. I was going to be there to watch my babies grow up and raise them.

But what was I thinking! I still had a drug problem. What was I going to do? I can't be a good momma addicted to dope.

Little did I know that on the day that I got arrested in February 2008, my parents and daughters had decided to tell me that they were going to let me go. That they were not going to let me come home back and forth anymore because it was hurting them too much.

I thank God they were not able to come and deliver that message to me. I believe I would have killed myself that day. To know my daughters were giving up on me. Them willing to live without me is devastating. But it was true—they had been living like I wasn't there. I hadn't been in their lives 100 percent. They couldn't depend on me.

Being on the streets is not easy. Being out on the streets as a woman and selling dope isn't either. People (men) thought they could take advantage of me. I hated the *b* word. I had been called that by abusive, cheating men, and I refused to let anyone call me that, even when playing around. One time, a guy had called me that, and I had two close acquaintances grab ahold of him. They took him to an abandoned home and beat him up pretty bad. They called me on the phone and asked if I wanted them to kill him. I said no. I just wanted him to apologize to me. I couldn't have a heart out there, and I didn't! So I was tough and mean; my heart was hard. I never allowed anyone to get close to me. There were some who caught feelings for me, but you never know why they are trying to love you. And all I wanted was to love my babies. I wanted to be with my babies. But I didn't love myself, and I was never going to be good for them until I did.

What have Odessa and Vinessa been going through? They have been growing up dealing with not only not having their dad but also not having their mom. Through my actions, I had taught them to run or quit when they had a problem. Not only run or quit but also run to drugs or alcohol. They had to face each day with issues of abandonment. Rejection, feelings of not enough, fear, resentment, disappointment, and hurt—all these dark spirits were hovering over my children. The sad thing is that I wasn't there to help them! I wasn't there when they were battling these demons! I wasn't there. The same way I didn't have the knowledge and tools to defeat Satan, neither did they. Satan loves to divide homes. He loves to destroy families, and he was destroying mine. While he was working to steal all my life away, he was also working on destroying my children.

No! I wanted to be an example to my daughters. I wanted to show them how strong their momma was. I wanted to show them how great a momma I really was. I wanted to hold them. I wanted to be there with them every day. I wanted to kiss my babies and tell them how much I love them, that they were my whole world, and that I would do anything for them!

I was a great momma when drugs weren't in the picture. What pain did I cause my parents? What pain did I cause my brothers? Drug addiction or alcoholism affects everyone whether we want to believe it or not. Our family and loved ones are watching us destroy our lives. They either enable us to continue to use, or the family shows tough love. When our family continues to give us money due to the lies we use for the need of money, they aren't helping us. They are giving us the ability to keep destroying our lives. They are never letting us fall or hit rock bottom. They always come to the rescue when they should let us fall. If we never fall, when will we reach out to God to save us? If our family and friends continue to enable us, when will our eyes open to what is really going on? We will never feel the need to cry out to God to save us. My family decided to show tough love. I am glad they did. It hurt me at the time because they wouldn't help me, but it was the right thing to do.

CHAPTER 14

How Beautiful Is God

I had always vowed to love my baby girls—to protect them. How could I allow drugs and money to rule me? How could I let those things rule my decisions? How could I let them take control over me? But it wasn't me. It was a demonic attack on my life. It was Satan's plan to kill me, to destroy my life and my future, and to steal my children from me. He found the right time to come into my life, and I allowed him to. And because he knows our weaknesses, he knew exactly what to put in my path every time. He knew who to use to hurt me, and it worked every time.

I didn't always sell drugs. There was a time I was just using. And man, when that drug is calling your name, it's in your thoughts. Your body wants it. Your body is craving it. It's hungry for it. And if you don't have the money to buy it, you are doing things you thought you would never do just to get some.

But how beautiful is God? A God who forgives a sinner like me. A God who loves me no matter what I had become.

There were times I would immediately give a small bag of dope to someone who just got out of jail. They would say, "Hey, I just got out." So I would give it to them like some kind of reward. But in actuality, I was giving that person death. Think about it. This person is clean of dope, and here I was, handing them something that was going to destroy them. I didn't start thinking this way until later. I didn't start thinking this way until my eyes were open.

Once I got saved, I asked God to forgive me for selling drugs to people. I was hurting someone's son or daughter, destroying someone's mom, dad, sister, or brother. I had an opportunity to run into a few people I used to sell to. I asked them to forgive me, that I was wrong. They said not to worry about it; if they didn't buy it from me, they would have bought it from someone else.

I'm telling you, my heart used to be black. I was mean. I didn't care about anyone. Like I said, I didn't care about myself. I didn't care because I couldn't be the momma and woman I was supposed to be. I was a soldier for the enemy. There were times I would be in a house with parents and kids. I'd be there selling dope to their mom and dad. I would feel bad that those kids were seeing their parents getting high. I bought a few groceries for them to eat. I've even paid their light bill because they would rather buy the dope. But again, I wasn't going to be too kind. I couldn't be there for my own babies. Why am I going to be there for theirs?

All the while that I am making mistakes and bad choices, God was there. He was aligning things up for me. He had heard every prayer my daughters had prayed. He had collected every one of their tears that they had shed for me. He was there. He was there comforting my babies. He was there while they cried themselves to sleep. He had a plan! God had a plan for my daughters and for me! But because I wasn't ready, I had to go through more bad stuff before really being ready to change.

Odessa & Vinessa fighting in prayer with faith in God,
that He would return their Momma back to them delivered
& set free from all the chains of the enemy

CHAPTER 15

Beat and Broken

I had moved to H-Town. It was getting too hot in our little town. And honestly, I thought it was going to be smooth. I thought I was going to be able to sell dope like I did in Alvin. But boy, was I wrong. I thought because everyone knew me in Alvin, I could go to Houston and sell just as good as I did in Alvin.

I can't tell you how many times I got jumped by dudes for my dope. I mean beat down. Stomping on my head and body. And there I went to my drug connection to tell him what happened and if he could give me more dope on credit. Who does that? He would give me some on credit, but after me coming to him with the same story so many times, he stopped. And once I didn't have any dope to sell or barely any money to buy more to flip, I ended up in houses where women would be pimped out. I quickly left those places. I ended up in a house where they tried to keep me as a prisoner. I don't know how I was able to get out of there, but the man left the house one day, so I was able to escape. I was out there in the streets living out of a hotel room trying to hustle daily to make enough money to eat, have a place to stay, and of course, get me some dope. I was crying one night walking the streets of Houston, and a man drove up next to me pretending to be an EMS. He offered to give me a ride, so I got in his car, and he forced me to do something I am ashamed of. He had a gun to my head, so I had no choice. He wanted to kill me, but he said something wouldn't let him, so he let me go.

I don't know why I didn't leave Houston the first time they beat and robbed me. I don't know why I didn't go back home the first time they raped me. I don't know why I always had to be so hardheaded! Why did I think that I could be out there in the streets by myself trying to be big time? But I was never scared.

I was so lost. I was so broken inside. I was so blind. I was full of anger and unforgiveness. All the reasons to be angry about my life were just adding up. All these people hurting me. All this disappointment of who I had become, all the things I was putting myself through all the rejection and all the pain and loneliness. My life had spiraled out of control. My spirit had cried out to God, and He always answered—with jail. One early morning after being beat up, I walked to a church about five miles away—on Fuqua Street in Houston. I cried all the way there. I walked in dirty with no shoes on. I cried as I listened to the preacher. When they asked for offering and tithes, I went up and took the gold chain I was wearing. And then I left. I knew God was working in my life even then.

If you read in the Bible, He would oftentimes put His people in captivity. Captivity is an opportunity for us to stop and realize what our life has become. Captivity is an opportunity to seek God with no distractions. It is a chance for a new start. But I *never* allowed God to speak to me while I was locked up. I never really gave Him an opportunity to change my life. I wouldn't give Him a chance to work in me.

Sure, I would request a black Holy Bible every time I went in. And yeah, I would read it and underline verses I knew. And yes, I would attend the church services helped by volunteer chaplains. But I never gave God a chance. I never gave myself a chance.

CHAPTER 16

God Had a Different Plan

In 2006, I signed for probation and three months in rehab. I was excited about going to rehab. The classes I attended helped me to evaluate my life and address the underlining issues from my past. I began to heal and start forgiving the ones who hurt me and let me down. I was also able to ask for forgiveness from the ones I had hurt along the way, like my daughters, parents, and brothers.

I had already been in the county for a few months, then got transferred to the rehab in Angleton. I could admit I was letting the program work for me, and I was working it. I was also getting closer to the Lord. When I was released from there, in my mind, I thought I was better and ready to face the world. But that only lasted a little while. I was back on the streets in a matter of five months.

My hair had gotten so long it was beautiful. A gentleman from the church we were attending liked me and vice versa. We ended up getting engaged. It only lasted a little while because the moment he told me no, I was gone. No one was going to tell me what I could or couldn't do. So there I went—to what I knew.

Little did I know I would be out on the streets for another two years before I get my life together. Dang, it! If I had only learned my lesson that time, I wouldn't have wasted more time.

In December 2007, the judge told me that if he saw me in his courtroom one more time, he was going to sentence me to ten years in prison. I said, "Yes, sir!" Two months later, in February 2008, I was arrested again. I was so angry that I got caught. I asked Mrs. Love to put me in solitary confinement so that I could get my mind prepared to do a lot of time. I skinned bald my head because I was fixing to do time my way; and that meant getting me a girlfriend. I was so angry! I refused to ask for a Bible this time. I told my parents not to wait for me and that I was going to come out worse than the way I went in.

Normally, once the Alvin Police Dept. put their cuffs on me, I was always more than happy to go in. Brazoria County was like a candy store to me because of the girls, and I loved the biscuits. I had been attracted to females for years but never really acted on it until later in my twenties. Being in jail with nothing but females made it easy to entertain the feelings of homosexuality. I had my share of flirty relationships not just in jail but on the outside as well. It wasn't something I spoke about to anyone, especially my family. I was raised to believe that homosexuals wouldn't enter the kingdom of God. I did pursue short-time relationships while in the county to help pass the time.

This time, when the cuffs were put on me, I was angry, not happy like before. I had just set up everything on the outside so I would never have to sell on the streets again. Man, I know now that God was saving me. He knew that this time was going to be different for me.

So I was on the wall, in solitude. I was alone, with no paper, no Bible, just me and four walls. I had one bed, one toilet, a stand-up shower, and one metal door with a very small glass window. That little window also has a door; it gets open when the guards need to talk to me. I had one sink connected to the toilet and a mirror, which was a steel plate bolted to the wall so I could see my reflection. There was a desk attached to my bed.

And there I was, just me and my thoughts. Days passed by, weeks passed by, and April 2008 came. On April 17, a volunteer chaplain left a small magazine on the outside of my metal door. A guard opened my door to hand me this *In Touch Magazine* by Charles Stanley. As I opened this small book, I began to read "The Dangers of Drifting."

> Unless we stay on course, we're going to pay the consequences. #1 *Your consequences become*

numb: When you start drifting, you begin to ignore your consequences. At first, your internal warning system pricks you, letting you know something isn't right. It sends you a message, then another one. But you continually excuse what you're doing and where you're headed. You ignore the cautions. Gradually, you desensitized your conscience so that it no longer bothers you. When that happens, you're headed for difficulty. #2 *You step out of God's will*: As you begin to drift, you step out of the Lord's will into a life of sin. This may sound harsh, but choosing to walk away from the truth of God's Word amounts to setting foot into some type of transgressions. Just because your conscience isn't blaring does not mean that the behavior or activity is okay. Once you've trusted Jesus as your Savior, you know that the Holy Spirit is there, deep within. You can deaden yourself to the fact that you can't even hear Him, but when that's the case, you are in serious trouble. #3 *You shrink away from spiritual things*: What happens is simple and natural; you start living in denial. If your conscience bothers you, you rationalize your behavior. 1 John 2:28 says, "Now, little children, abide in Him, so that when He appears, we may have confidence and not shrink away from Him in shame at His coming." Why would you shrink away from things in the Christian life that are meant to bring us joy and happiness? Because you're off course. #4 *You lose your ability to hear Him*: You won't ever lose your salvation, but you can fall into the sin of unbelief (Hebrews 3:12) and lose your capacity to hear God. The farther you fall away, the less you're going to hear. And the longer you are adrift, the more difficult it will be for you to hear.

Without an anchor in Christ, it's easy to invite destructive thoughts and habits that blur your vision of God and deafen your ear to Him. #5 *You suffer internally, if not externally*: When you choose to let go of your fellowship with God, and when you cease reading the Word and attending church, you change physically, emotionally, mentally and spiritually—every aspect of your life is affected. As you wander away from what you know to be important, you will experience guilt, which brings about tension and stress. Then the more you linger without direction, the harder you will have to work to cover the guilt—especially if you live around somebody who is very godly. Consider, for example, a righteous wife whose husband ventures into immortality. Every time he comes home, he feels guilty. Stress mounts. His sin causes tension and anxiety; guilt brings about anger and hurt. The deceitfulness of sin is like termites inside of him, eating away at his peace and contentment. #6 *Your drifting grieves God's heart.* The Bible talks about "grieving the Spirit" (Eph. 4:30). A lot of people wander away from the Lord, thinking they have everything under control. But horrible destruction can occur in their life because there's an unavoidable penalty for drifting from God. And it grieves His heart more than we know. #7 *You miss God's best.* What kind of plan does the heavenly Father have for you? The best plan possible because He loves you very much! Yet unfortunately, believers sometimes drift at the most strategic time in their life- they can actually be distracted by how well things are going. A person can be healthy, successful in relationships, and thriving financially. But he can drift right by an awesome opportunity if he isn't tuned into what God is trying to do in his life. Do you want God's best? What are you doing to get it? Perhaps you think, *Maybe one of these days, things will just work out.* But things don't "just work out." We have to make an effort to follow the Lord and listen carefully to His wisdom. #8 *You push away those who love you most.* The drifting process leads you farther and farther from where you should be, until you don't even want to go back. At that point, you've lost your sense of where you are spiritually. You don't hear God anymore or sense His presence. That is a terrible place to be! What's more, sailing along without direction changes a person. When your relationship with God is affected, so are your actions-you may spend your money in different ways and your time with different people. You may alter how you make decisions and rethink your likes, dislikes, preferences, and prejudices. Sadly, when you walk away from God, you may push away the people He has put into your life to love and care for you. #9 *You have a negative impact on others.* The Lord wants us to be the salt and light, so He disciplines us when we go astray (Heb. 12:6–8, 10). If you don't think you have an impact on anybody else, think again. You do. When the husband/father in the family drifts, it affects everybody in that household, often leading the children down an unhealthy path. And what about other authorities-such as teachers, employers, and public figures? When they deviate from righteousness, the people who admire or hope to please them tend to follow suit. It's important to ask yourself, *What kind of impact am I having on those around me?* #10 *You leave your life in ruins.* There's one last consequence

> of drifting: You make shipwreck of your life. Sometimes a believer will make such poor decisions that even though God forgives him, his life may never be what he had hoped. God willing, that won't happen and thankfully, the Lord can pick up the pieces of your life, no matter how broken you are. The Bible gives us a clear warning about wandering away from righteousness. Now is a good time to take an honest look at your life. If you are drifting, I pray that you will be wise enough to stop and let God put you back on course for His best all the days of your life. ("Dangers of Drifting")

As I kept reading, everything it was talking about was me. I just wept. I fell to my knees, and I cried out to God! Every word I read was speaking about me! I had drifted away from God. I had stepped away from God's will. Little by little, I had begun to ignore the voice of the Lord. Not only ignore it, but I had pushed Him away that I couldn't hear Him any longer. Every choice, every sin, every decision I had made was killing me on the inside and the outside. When I turned my back on my Father, I broke His heart. I had betrayed His love. I was missing out on all of God's best for my life. I had pushed everyone who loved me away! My actions were having a negative impact on my daughters. My life was in ruins! I couldn't help but cry. I had destroyed my life. But God, at this moment, was calling me to return to Him so He could put it all back together.

> Forgive me, Father. Forgive me for all of my sins. I know You created me for something better than this! For more than this! I am so tired of wearing orange! I am so tired of watching my daughters grow up behind a glass window! I am so tired of my children growing up without me! I am so tired of destroying my life! *Please*, don't let me leave prison until You say that I am ready!

You created me. You know how long it will take
for me to really change. I rededicate my life to
You. Come into my heart and be Lord of my life.

Then I got up and walked up to my mirror and asked myself for forgiveness for everything I put myself through.

It is very important to not only receive Jesus into our hearts and receive His forgiveness. It is very important to also forgive ourselves because the enemy loves to bring up our past. He wants to remind us of all our mistakes. He wants us to continue to live in guilt and shame.

I realized I had been hurting myself all of these years for the actions of others. I realized that I had to take responsibility for all the choices and decisions I had made. Sin will take you further than you want to go. Sin will cost you more than you are willing to pay. Sin will keep you longer than you want to stay.

(Dad) Rudy, (Mom) Rebecca, Odessa, Vinessa & Trudy they were visiting me in TDC Huntsville Unit October 2009

CHAPTER 17

Cheating Is a Betrayal of Love

The times I was cheated on were cruel. There were men in my life that said they loved me but, behind my back, went to the bed of another woman. It was a betrayal of love. It was all a game. It was a betrayal of trust. I gave myself to these relationships, and they betrayed me. I would open myself to them for them to be in the arms of another woman. So many lies were told so that they were able to sneak out. So many lies were told to cover the truth of their real location.

Lies were said to explain why money was missing. Lots of times, my friends and family knew about the cheating and never said a word. And for me to be invested in a relationship to only find out it was all a lie is devastating! I go back in my thoughts, trying to figure out when he was really with her, trying to remember if the time he said he was at work, he was really with her. I would find out my cheating partner made it a habit to lie. The cheating would break me! It would make me feel insecure. The cheating would make me feel like something was wrong with me. The different cheating relationships ruined my trust for any man. It would be hard to go into the next relationship without thinking this one may cheat too. It would make me automatically assume he was going to run to another woman. I hated feeling that way because it would make me so jealous. I had to ask God to help me, to remove the jealousy from me. I had to ask God to help me so that I could rebuild my self-esteem and confidence.

Once I let Him into my life, He showed me the love He had for me and gave me a reassurance that He would never hurt me. I had to work on letting go of the "all men are the same" mindset. I had to learn how to love myself. I had to learn and realize I didn't deserve to be cheated on. I had to realize it wasn't because I did something wrong, but it was because of the wrong choices my partner made. And lots of times, they only felt bad about the cheating because they got caught. Lots of times, they continued to lie once they were caught because they didn't want to accept the consequences of their actions.

I want you to know that every time we sin, we are betraying the love of God. He loves us all so much He willingly allowed His Son to die a gruesome death for each of us, so when we intentionally sin against Him, that hurts Him. I have had my share of one-sided relationships, where I give and give and give and all they do is take and take and take. It is a one-sided relationship. The love is coming from one side. The commitment is coming from one side. The honesty and work are coming from one side. And the money is coming out from one side. It isn't cool at all. It's called being used—used for everything you can give them, used for all they can take from you.

Well, sometimes we are that way to God. We are ready to take and take from Him, and we are not willing to give any of ourselves to Him in return. We treat Him like a genie. We promise that if He does something for us, we will do something for Him, and it shouldn't be like that. It doesn't work that way. He wants a relationship with us, with you. When we surrender our lives over to Christ, we get so much! The world gives this artificial joy and happiness, but it isn't real. This world gives temporary peace and satisfaction. I searched the world for joy and happiness. I searched for peace, and I never found it. I never found the answer out there in the world. I tried to fill my void with money, partying, people, drugs, material things, men, sex, but they were never enough.

All those things were never enough because I always needed more to refill the void again. They were like Band-Aids that never fixed the real issue. I am nothing without God. If God isn't in my life, I am living in vain. I could have my own agenda, but what matters is, did I fulfil God's agenda? I may have the great job, wonderful husband, good kids, and money, but my life will still be missing something. I will be missing God. He is the almighty God; all-knowing, sovereign God; He who gives life and breath to all things; the only One who can give true peace. It is up to me and you to stay connected to our Father, our Source of life. Once that relationship builds, it isn't that we have to stop doing the wrong things; we begin to not want to. Everything we will ever need is in Him. The Bible says that God is a Father to the fatherless. He will never abandon you. Our Abba Father, will never hurt you or disappoint you. He will defend you and protect you. He will stand up for you. He wants your attention. You will realize that He is always faithful to His Word. On this earth, we will have seasons, good and bad. But if you know that He is leading you, then you know anything going on in your life, He allowed it. And the times of difficulties, we either need to remove some character from ourselves, or He is testing our heart. He is testing our faith. So we rejoice because He will always deliver you! He has delivered you before, and He will deliver again! God, my Father, has satisfied my hunger and fulfilled my life. He has given me a purpose and a destiny.

God has a purpose and destiny for you. You have the ability to live, walk, talk, and respond in victory every time because you know that God will always come through for you.

I know now that my God will always deliver me. He will always save me. He will always come through for me. He will always make a way for me when there seems to be no way. He will always do the miraculous for me. And if I know that He is with me, then I can rest, knowing He will come through for me time and time again. I can regulate my life from a place of peace because I know that God will always perfect everything that concerns me. Living for God was the best decision I ever made. And I know why the devil tries so hard to keep us from God.

The Bible says that the Lord is my Shepherd, I shall not want. That means nothing missing, nothing broken, I want for nothing! He makes me lie down in tender, pleasant places. He leads me beside peaceful, quiet, and restful places. I have no reason to fear! I have no reason to worry. He is the One who leads me. He is the One who guides and protects me. And so I am able to operate my life from a place of rest and ease. It is so easy to act or talk or think like the world does. But the Bible says, we are not of this world, so we reprogram ourselves to respond according to the way the Word says. We live according to what the Word says. We choose to believe only what God's Word says about each situation we face. What an honor to know we have access to God!

Because we have received Jesus Christ into our hearts, we now have the privilege to go directly to the Creator of the world! I have looked out into the sky and saw the wonders of His creative hands, painting His beautiful pictures. He has designed galaxies and every species. Out of everything in the world, you are His most special masterpiece. You, He values above all things. There is no good thing He will withhold from you, the Bible says. Our God is an awesome God!

CHAPTER 18

I Am Guilty of Everything I've Ever Done

I have learned so much because of everything that I have gone through. I know I shouldn't regret any of it because they were all my choices. I am not happy with a lot of the decisions I made, but they were mine. I do wish I could do things over again. But I am who I am today because of all my choices. I am most proud of myself when I began to take responsibility for my own actions. I began to allow God to heal me. I began to think before making any decision. I learned to think before I responded. I began to live a healthy, sober, godly life. I wasn't blaming anyone anymore for my actions or behavior. Once I did this, I was free! Free from being a victim, and on a path to being a victor!

I do wish I learned a lot sooner. But today, I take advantage of the opportunity to share with others my testimony. I no longer make choices that hurt me, *thinking*, I'm hurting the ones who hurt me. I yearn to be a leader by example everywhere I go, especially to my children.

For so many years, I destroyed myself for all the bad that had happened to me. Every day, it was a constant reminder of what each and every abuser had done to me while they slept well at night.

A person has two choices in life, they can live their life in turmoil, hate, and sadness because of their upbringing. Or they can choose to live better. Just like my girls, they could have used me and their dad as an excuse to ruin their lives. Or they could say, "I want to be better than them." And that is what I always told them. Even now, I want them to be better than me.

Vinessa and Odessa have both turned out to be beautiful, talented, and smart women. They are wonderful mommas to their babies. I am so very proud of them. I am blessed to have them.

A diamond must endure extreme pressure, and gold must go through extreme heat to remove impurities. So when we endure these difficult times, embrace them. We are each on a journey, a race. There are characteristics that need to be removed from our lives so that we can be all that God intended us to be. You were made with treasure inside. If not, why does Satan try so hard to destroy us? No one robs an empty house. He is trying to steal all that God has for you. You are so special. And you are so strong. God designed each of us unique. Don't waste time trying to be like someone else; there is no one else in this world just like you.

Sometimes we don't see anything good about ourselves. You think you are not funny or that you are unattractive. You may not have any friends. You are blind to the truth of who you really are. If you are a Christian, you are a child of God. You are an heir to His kingdom! You are no longer a foreigner but a citizen of heaven. Our name is written in the Book of Life. You have been given power from on high! God gave His children the ability to live a successful, healthy, prosperous, and peaceful life here on earth! You are the apple of God's eyes. Your name is written on His hands, where they nailed Him to the cross. He sees the very best in you. He sees you as holy and righteous.

He can take a drug addict, convict, dirty, angry, and mean girl like me and see the best in me. And He sees the very best in you too. He wants His very best for you. Lots of times, we are distracted by all the things going around we miss Him. We are blinded to see what matters most—Him.

For some of us, it takes longer to get on the right path. For some, it takes longer to realize we are on the wrong path. We have to be tired of the way we are choosing to live and finally accept we are lost without God. I want you to know it is never too late to change. It is never too late with God. Never! As long as you have air in your lungs, there is time. But don't wait until the last minute. Enjoy living for Jesus. Enjoy all the benefits of being a child of the King! It is a life full of blessings and power! You will have the ability to change any situation that comes your way. You will never have to face any storm alone because you will have the Holy Spirit. As you get closer to God, as you read the Bible, you are being built up in His Word. You are discovering all that you are, all that God meant for you, and you are able to go through anything without difficulty.

My time in prison was an opportunity to seek God and get the knowledge I needed from His Word. Everything that caused me to go to prison was waiting for me. And so to ensure I would never go back to the ways of the world, I studied and studied the Bible. You can do the same. Use whatever situation you are in at this moment to seek God. Start right where you are at! And watch Him restore your life. He will return everything back to you that the devil stole from you.

I want to encourage you to always be growing but in the right things—in the things of God. The Holy Spirit will guide you; just ask Him. Ask Him where He wants you to live or if you should go back to school. Ask Him about a job or vehicle. He wants to be involved in your life.

IT'S NEVER TOO LATE

God has restored my life. He has returned everything back better than before

CHAPTER 19

Thank You, Mom and Dad

I can only imagine how my actions affected my parents. We never realize that our actions have consequences, good or bad. And oftentimes we think the choices we make only affect us, but they don't. They affect everyone. I know I hurt my mom and dad. They probably blamed themselves for everything I did. And had thoughts of "I should have done this" or "I could have done that" to avoid all of this. In all actuality, it all happened exactly the way it was supposed to. I had an opportunity to ask them to forgive me. I was wrong in my choices and the way I handled everything.

So if I can give any advice here, just love your parents. Love on them. Hug them, kiss them, sit on their laps, or let your mom run her fingers through your hair. Our parents are not given manuals. And they are raising their children the way they were taught. Now I am not condoning bad behavior or abuse. Definitely not! And it's definitely not an excuse if they were raised wrongly, and then they do it to their children. Again, every person has a choice—to be just like their parents or be better than them. That is how the generation curses happen. Someone has to break the cycle. If your parents didn't hug you, hug your kids. If your parents talked negatively to you, speak positive to your children. We have to break the cycle! If your parents were abusive, choose not to do it to your children. If your parents were drug addicts or alcoholics, choose not to be! The curses of the generations are demons, and we have to break that legal right for them to be there. The reason demons are there and have been tormenting families for generation after generation is that no one has told them to leave! We have to say, "I break the legal rights of drug addiction or bipolar. I break the legal rights of pornography or depression. I rebuke you, Satan, and your demons from my life and my children's lives in the name of Jesus and cast you into the abyss." If we never confront the enemy, he will stay because we gave him a right to be there.

If you have broken bridges with your parents or a resentment or anger toward them, I want you to sit down and pray. Ask God to give you the words to say to them. Pray that they will receive your words with love. Pray that your parents will sit down and listen to what you have to say. Remember to choose your words accordingly. Say your words in a manner that will get you the results you want. If you go in there angry and yelling every word, you are not going to achieve anything. Have a talk with your parents. Don't allow the enemy to keep division in your family. Let them know what their actions did to you. Let them know what their words made you feel. Let them know. They need to know. We need to speak up and quit burying it on the inside because it will kill us. We want God to heal that area of our life. We want God to mend our hearts and completely restore that hurt we have been carrying for so long so that we can move forward. The longer we carry that hurt, we give room to the enemy to play with us and use it to destroy us on the inside.

I had to learn to forgive my mom for the things she did and forgive my dad for the things he did. They made a lot of mistakes, but so did I. God forgave me of mine, so I must forgive them of theirs. It isn't easy to forgive someone when they continually do the things you are wanting to forgive them from. But I knew I didn't want to carry that in my heart anymore. I learned that I cannot change anyone and the person must want to change for themself.

I love my mom and dad. I know that all the strict rules when I was growing up were to protect me. And I know that while I was living on the streets, they were protecting my daughters from me. I know my parents did their best to raise my daughters, and I am so grateful for that. They could have easily said that I would have to be responsible for them, but they didn't. And for that, I will love them forever.

Again, I am totally against parents abusing their children or allowing others to abuse their children, but I am agreeing with old-fashioned raising. I do believe all children need discipline, correction, guidance, love, and protection. All children respond to discipline differently, some with a spanking, some with a lecture, but we as parents learn our children and know what works best with each child. Proverbs 29:15 says, "A child left to himself brings shame to his mother." Proverbs 13:24 says, "He who spares his rod hates his son, but he who loves him disciplines him promptly."

When my daughters finally came home to live with me, I received full custody of them! God is so good. I wanted to raise my children differently from the way I was raised. Yes, I would spank them, but only when it was necessary. I would always correct them with the Word of God (the Holy Bible). Whatever situation it was, I would refer back to what God's Word said about it. We would talk first. If I was upset, I would go to my room and pray first because I never wanted to talk or yell at them in anger. I never wanted to hurt them with my words. I never wanted to hurt my daughters. But I did want them to see that their actions had consequences. Using the Word gave them the ability to see what exactly they did wrong. Sometimes I would take their phone away or ground them for a little while. But I always spoke to my daughters. I wanted to keep that door open for them to be able to talk to me. I did my best to love my babies, kiss them, and hug them every day. To know that I was told I would never get them back and then for God to answer my prayers, I was so grateful! I was given the opportunity to show my daughters how much I loved them. I was able to show them that we don't run away from storms. We run to Jesus! We should never discipline or spank in anger but with love. I would always hug them afterward and tell them that I love them. Children are a gift from God. We are responsible for them. God is entrusting them to us so we will raise them up in the Lord.

(Dad) Rudy, (Mom) Rebecca, Odessa & Vinessa

CHAPTER 20

Learning How to Stand on God's Word

May 2008, I knew I had run from God for years, living however I wanted to, but the moment I asked Jesus Christ into my heart and received His forgiveness, His Blood washed away all of my sins and the sins I didn't remember. I was now born again! I was now a Child of God, washed white as snow. I was a brand-new creature and had a new future ahead of me. It happened immediately. And it can happen in an instant for anyone who does the same.

I had remembered the judge had previously said that if he saw me in his courtroom again, he was going to give me ten years in prison. So in my heart and mind, I knew that prison sentence didn't belong to me anymore because God had forgiven my past. I knew I still needed to pay the consequence for my crimes, but I wasn't going to accept ten years. So I invited God into the situation. I opened my Bible and looked for a scripture. As I read it, I put my name in it. And I advise you to do the same for any situation. When you read, put your name in it or the name of a person you are praying for. This helped me learn how to pray better and taught me how to speak with wisdom when I would minister to others. And so I would confess the scripture over myself. I would confess that I was forgiven of all of my sins, and I would thank God for what He had done for me and for what He was going to do for me.

This all happened over a time of two to three months as I stood on God's Word. Colossians 2:14 which says, "Having wiped out the handwriting of requirements that was against us, which was contrary to us. And He has taken it out of the way, having nailed it to the cross. Having disarmed principalities and powers, He made a public spectacle of them, triumphing over them in it." Praise God! You see what that verse says? Every written thing contrary to us, He nailed to the cross! So I daily meditated on that verse. I would stir up my spirit, and I received and believed His Word! Hallelujah!

When my attorney came to visit me, she said she had spoken to the district attorney and got my sentence down to seven years. I said, "No, I am not doing seven years." I knew that I was guilty of my crimes. I knew I had to face the consequences of my actions. But my Creator was involved now! The next time I received a visit from my attorney, she said she got it dropped down to five years. I told her that I wasn't signing for five. The next time she came to see me, she said, "I got your time down to three years TDC and eighteen months State Penitentiary."

I said, "I'll sign!"

Now when you find a scripture that pertains to your situation and you're confessing it and believing it for yourself, that is standing on the Word of God. You are locking your feet in it. You are firm in that Word you are declaring. You are rooted in it. You are grounded in it! And no matter what you see and no matter what you hear, you stand strong in the Word spoken. The Bible, the Word of God, is living and powerful and sharper than any two-edged sword, piercing even to the division of soul and spirit and of joints and marrow, and is a discerner of the thoughts and intents of the heart (Hebrews 4:12). God's Word is powerful! And when we speak His Word, it never returns void! He had already shown me that He is faithful to His Word when I believed for my sentence to get dropped.

I knew that if God came through for me before, He would do it again! I knew that when you are on God's path, He will always come through time and time again. We just have to trust and believe. I had come upon a scripture saying, "I will return your children back to you and bring you back to the land I promised your fathers." So I held onto that verse. I would remind God of that verse. God was going to return my children back to me and place us where we were supposed to be. For months, weeks, and days, I confessed that scripture. Even when I got home from prison, I believed in my heart what He had said! I had been paroled to my parents' house. At first, they lived in a small two-bedroom apartment when I moved in. Can you believe they decided to move into a bigger place so I could fit? My parents didn't have to do that. I had so many classes that I was required to complete and parole visits I was required to go, but I didn't expect them to bend over backward to help me. I couldn't expect them to change their schedules for me. I had put myself in that situation, so it was up to me to fulfil them. But my parents took a chance, not knowing if this time would be like all the others, and they opened their home to me. There were times the words "you are never getting your daughters back" were said to me. And it hurt me. The old me would have been ready to yell back, but instead, I would go to my room and pray. I would remind God and myself what He said about returning my children to me.

I was going on thirty months of being a Christian. This was amazing to me because my life had truly changed. Everyone could see it! I was putting to practice the Word I had learned and studied in prison. It was evident in my life I was serving the Lord. I met JP immediately after I got out of prison at a church in La Marque, Texas. I thought I had recognized him sitting on the third row but wasn't too sure, so I didn't say anything. After the church service, as he was walking out, he recognized me and made his way to where me and my family were standing. We both caught up on a few things because we had known each other prior to this moment. We had both known each other in the world. We had a relationship for a short time, and yes, drugs were involved. I remember sitting in his truck one day, looking over at him and knowing that he was missing Jesus, but I didn't offer Him too him because I was pretty lost myself. So as we were talking right there at the end of the church service, he invited me to Brazoria County Jail to go minister with him. Immediately I said yes! He told me how he needed to go to prison to find Jesus. So I started going every Sunday morning to BCDC to minister the Word and sing! I loved it! I was able to give hope to these women who were just like me. I inspired them because they could see the change in me, and they knew they could have it too. And as JP and I would spend time together, we began to have feelings for each other. At that time me, my brother Gabriel, Odessa, and a few other guys started a band called Dayz of Mercy. We would travel to different churches. We would sing songs that I had written in prison. It was awesome! At the time, JP and I were hanging out a whole lot. He was being tempted by the enemy because he didn't want to sin against God with me. So he disappeared. He wouldn't call, and he wouldn't answer my calls. He wouldn't respond to any of my text messages. And he broke my heart. I continued with the band, visiting churches and sharing my testimony, but my heart was broken. A member of my brother Gabriel's church named Gary told me that God told him to help me get a car, so I got a white Dodge Magnum! I loved my car! I was also going to cosmetology school in La Marque, Texas, so I could one day work and support myself and my daughters. I was doing really well when I got out. I had put only three things on my to-do list. Not like all the other times I was released from jail, this time, I was going to do things the right way. I was getting an education. I was going to church and living with my parents and daughters. I want to tell you it was always a challenge for me when I would live with them. The enemy would use my mother to hurt me with her words. She didn't know how to talk to me, and when she would, she would always hurt me. I don't think she would pray before talking to me. I don't think she stopped to think first about what she was going to say because if she had, she would have gotten the results she wanted. This time when I was released and came home to live with my parents was different. I didn't argue back. I know that my mother loved me. She was the one who made sure I received a letter in the mail in prison once a week. She made sure my daughters would write me once a week. I had trained myself to run to God when storms came, so that's what I would do—go to my room and fight through prayer. I didn't fight physically anymore. I fought in the Spirit!

    After living with my parents for eight months, I just couldn't do it anymore. I couldn't live in that environment, so I moved out. I had moved in with JP. He came back into the picture about two months before. He apologized for disappearing. He felt the best way for the enemy not to tempt him was to stay away from me. Although he was sorry for doing that to me, I kept that hurt deep in my heart. After school, I would pick up Odessa and Vinessa. They would spend the day and evening with me, and then I would drop them off at my parents.

October 2010, as I was getting the girls ready to take them back to my parents, Vinessa said, "Momma, I want to come live with you."

So I told her, "Let's pray!"

We prayed that when she told them that she wanted to live with me, my mom and dad would be sensitive to the Holy Spirit and know that it was time. I hugged Vinessa real hard.

The next day, when I spoke to my mom, she said, "Vinessa asked me if she can go live with you."

I said, "What did you say?"

My momma told me that she and Vinessa packed up all her belongings and that she was going to let her live with me. I *cried*! The day had finally come! I thanked God for answering Vinessa and my prayer. I thanked God for healing and mending that bridge. I thanked God that my parents finally realized it was time for me to have my children back. I thanked God because not only did my parents trust me but my baby girl did too! At this time, JP and I had moved out of his momma's house and moved into my brother Rudy's apartment in Alvin. We were taking over his lease because he and Gabriel were moving to Clearlake. So my daughter was coming home! We continued to pick up Odessa every day after school. Vinessa was living with us already two months when Christmas vacation came for the kids at school. Odessa stayed with us the whole time. We had so much fun. I can't explain the joy in my heart to have my babies with me. JP and I gave them such a wonderful Christmas and their new mamaw, Linda. She was so sweet to us. She accepted me and my girls right away, and so did JP. When Christmas break was over, it was time to send Odessa back with my mom and dad. And she said she didn't want to go back. She said she wanted to stay with me. Oh my goodness! My children had returned to me, and God had us right where He wanted. I thank God my parents saw the change in me and chose to trust me again. And my daughters, I was so grateful to God they were ready to be with their momma. I couldn't help but cry! All the years, I had yearned and cried for my daughters to be with me, all the years of heartache being away from them. All I ever wanted was them. All I ever wanted was them to be with me. I wanted them to be proud of me. And that day had finally come! I was going to have my daughters living with me.

God is so amazing! All my praise goes to God! You see, the Bible is real. The Word of God is alive, and when we take Him at His Word and believe it in our hearts, it surely comes to pass. The moment I gave my life to God, He began restoring my life. Little by little, my prayers were being answered one by one. Finally, my life was what I had always dreamed of it being. All I ever wanted was to be with my children, and I finally had them! It was all because I allowed God into my life. I allowed Him to lead me. When He is leading you, you are exactly where you are supposed to be and at the right time. When you trust God, He is working and moving everything for your good. He withholds no good thing from His children, and He had withheld no good from me. He wants to be in your life. He wants you to want Him in your life. The Bible says we are made by Him for Him. So when we live our lives away from Him, we are robbing ourselves of God's best for our lives. I learned from the beginning that when I truly trust Him and I have faith in what He has said in His Word, I will have the results of His Word.

If there is something you haven't invited God or His Word to be a part of, you should try it. When you have asked Jesus Christ into your heart and make Him Lord over your life, you are now a Child of God. Every Word, every blessing, and every promise written in the Bible belongs to you. You just have to believe. I want to share with you that everything we caused our family and our children, we can't expect everything to be easy! We burned a lot of bridges. We lost their trust and confidence. How many letters did we write home saying "this time it will be different" or "I've changed, and I'm better now"? We made so many empty promises to everyone, so we are the ones who have to earn that trust back. We have to be patient with them and ourselves. We have to prove to all of them that, this time, it is going to be different. We have to show them. Stop talking about it and be about it!

JP and I were raising my daughters in the Lord. There were many times he was very strict and very protective with my daughters, especially over Odessa. They had a good relationship, so she respected his opinions. Vinessa was not so easy to accept him; she just wanted me all to herself. He did his best to talk to them and pray with them. I wasn't traveling anymore with the band Dayz of Mercy, but I was still going to cosmetology school. One day, Miss Arlene, a volunteer chaplain who would go to Brazoria County Jail, reached out to me and invited me to her church at Christ Embassy. She was eager to introduce me to Pastor Daniel. And once I heard the Word spoken there, I knew that's where I wanted to get planted. I could see growth in me, in all of us. Odessa and I became praise and worship leaders. Odessa and Vinessa eventually became part of the sound team as well, running the video screens and cameras. Pastor Daniel would put my dad and JP to lead prayers before the service. My whole family followed us there. JP worked in the oil field so wasn't home too often. I needed to hear that I was loved every day. I needed to be hugged or felt loved daily. I needed kisses. Because he worked out of town so much, I didn't receive any of that affection. In the beginning of our marriage, we worked through it. We made it work. We video called every day. We called each other every day. I would tell him I needed that affection from him. But it seemed like my feelings didn't matter because no change was made. We found a property that was perfect for us. And the Lord let everything work in our favor. I was raising my daughters in the Lord and working at my new salon, Studio 7, in Alvin, Texas. It was awesome! God was growing my business. I had an established life with my babies, but I allowed the enemy to begin to whisper in my ear.

"You're alone. You're raising your daughters alone. He just comes home for sex and no affection. You're beautiful. Any man would love to kiss you."

I was faithful to my husband. After five years of no change, I just couldn't see myself living that way for the rest of my life. We should have sought godly counsel. I shouldn't have been moved by emotions. I really allowed the enemy to play games in my mind. I had the ability to shut the enemy up, but I failed. A few months before our fifth anniversary, I had tried one last time to see if any changes would be made, and my requests were swept under the rug. So my heart was tired. He was good to my girls and did what he knew to provide for our family, but I gave up. I decided to leave and left him everything. I wouldn't have been able to keep up with the house or truck note. And I started to sneak a drink here and sneak a drink there. I stepped down from praise and worship. And I stopped going to minister at Brazoria County. I felt drained. I was giving and pouring into so many areas that I felt like I wasn't getting anything in return. I felt like people were just taking and taking from me. Here is where we as believers must hold fast. We must not be led by our emotions. Emotions are fickle. We are to be led by the Spirit and not by the flesh. I should have locked myself in the room and prayed in tongues and rebuked Satan. We as believers have this magnificent light that surrounds us! We possess a power given to us from on high. We are the light in this world! Demons are under our feet! Sickness and disease are under our feet! God calls us to go and lay hands on the sick and heal them, so how can I possess depression? How could a believer possess loneliness, despair, sickness? Christians have the ability to have demons on the inside of us hiding without us knowing they are there. Deliverance is for the Christian. There are Christians who need to be delivered like I needed to be. I was a Christian and had a demon of divorce and a demon of loneliness and depression. But because I wasn't taught correctly, I didn't know to cast them out. Deliverance is not for a non-Christian. If you cast out a demon from a non-Christian, yes, the demon leaves; but because the person doesn't have Jesus inside them, nor do they have the Holy Spirit inside them, the demon comes back and brings seven more demons with him. The state of that person will be worse than before. So a person must get saved first, then they can be delivered from the demons. The Holy Spirit revealed to me that there are believers who, although they have this magnificent light and power, have their heads down. Why? Because they are not aware of who they are! They don't know the power they possess. They don't know that Satan and his demons and their attacks are under their feet! And they have the ability to be set free! God wants His people set free from every chain of bondage. God wants His children free of pain, sorrow, guilt, and shame. He wants us delivered from hidden secrets, past pain, and past disappointments. God allowed His Son, Jesus, to be beaten, tortured, and bruised for all that, and yet we continue to carry them. We don't have to be sad or have guilt or shame. We don't have to. He wants us to let it go. He died for it. Don't let His death be in vain. Accept His gift of liberty so that you can enjoy all the benefits of the cross. There is more to the cross than just salvation. There is healing, peace, and rest. There is power and joy! Don't allow Satan and his demons to steal any more of your time. We waste so much time holding on to pain or unforgiveness when He tell us not to. Enjoy your freedom!

CHAPTER 21

God Has a Plan for You

It doesn't matter if you are a Christian or don't have Christ as your Lord; life has problems. Life will have challenges, dilemmas, storms, and good times. But if you do have Jesus Christ, it makes life easier to go through it. So if we know that storms come, shouldn't we be prepared for them?

Like the men and women I minister to in jail, I tell them to study the Word of God and get strong in their faith and in their walk with God because everything that caused them to get locked up is waiting for them at the door. So we should prepare ourselves. Prepare ourselves for battle—a spiritual battle.

The enemy will definitely put things in our path to distract us. He wants us to get off the path God has for us. God has a calling for each of us. If we are off of that calling, we aren't actually living for the purpose we were created for. Our lives will be empty. We truly never have full gratification in the things we are involved with if we aren't living in the calling set for us by God. Acts 20:24 says, "But none of these things move me; nor do I count my life dear to myself, so that I may finish my race with joy, and the ministry which I received from the Lord Jesus, to testify to the gospel of the grace of God." We shouldn't be moved by negative situations in our lives when we have Christ Jesus. We should always have a sense of rest and peace—a reassurance that God is and will take care of us. And we should finish this race, this journey. We should finish the assignment God has given us and start fighting back! We need to stop allowing ourselves to be Satan's punching bag. We should rise up and use the authority God has given us here on this earth. Jesus punked Satan already. And Satan is angry about it and wants a rematch. So Jesus left us here to fight this round. The Bible says that God's people perish for the lack of knowledge. And that is true. We suffer or fall victim to all of Satan's schemes because we don't know either how to fight or know the tools to fight him with. But I am here to tell you to fight. Tell him that he isn't welcome in your home. Tell him he isn't welcome in your life. Tell him! Confront him. Confront his demons, call them out by name, and cast them out in the name of Jesus! And then throw them into the abyss to never return again! He has wasted and tried to destroy our lives for too long, and it has to stop now!

We need to have a relationship with the One who designed us. Building that relationship is vital for us during our time here on earth. You see, life here on earth is temporary. Our lives will live on for all of eternity forever and ever, in heaven or in hell. But everything we do here on earth determines where we will go. Death here on earth is not the end but the beginning of our afterlife.

So building that foundation here on earth with God is so important! You see, when Jesus resurrected, He left the Holy Spirit here to live in us. The Holy Spirit is our helper. He helps us, He guides us, and He leads us. He gives us the right advice and helps us make the right decisions. We never are alone because He lives and dwells inside us.

Of course, you have to receive Jesus into your heart by inviting Him in to be your Lord and Savior, and then ask the Holy Spirit

to come in to live in you. He comes with power and authority, which then you possess! You will have all authority to cast out demons, lay your hands on the sick, and minister His Word to others. You won't have to fall victim to any of Satan's schemes against you. You won't be an ordinary human being; you will be a super being, carrying all power and authority with you. And when you speak God's Word with confidence and with faith, it will accomplish what you send it out to do.

God would never just abandon His children without any power. The Bible says that we are equipped to handle any situation. His divine power has given us all things that pertain to life and godliness. Wealth, drugs, sex—all that this world offers could never bring true joy; they will never bring true fulfillment. There will always be a sense of emptiness. That's why a person (without Christ) has the need to want more and more because they think that will make them happy, but it will never be enough. Even an alcoholic or drug addict needs more and more; it will never be enough. Nothing, nothing on earth will fulfill a human being.

What they truly need is that connection with their Father God. That is why the Bible says, "See and taste that the Lord is good, blessed is the one who trusts Him." Matthew 5:6 says, "Blessed are those who hunger and thirst for righteousness, for they shall be filled."

We are in a spiritual battle every day. Satan and his demons don't sleep; they are relentless to steal the crown of glory from your head and keep you from entering heaven. They will do whatever they can to tempt you, disrupt your peace, and cause division in your life. They will use all kinds of tricks to lure you back and turn you away from God. Going to church on Sunday and midweek service is not enough. We have to study the Word and apply it to our lives. God is seeking a pure and Holy people. He is Holy; therefore, we, too, must be Holy. So we must purify our minds, purify our hearts, and sanctify our homes, not giving any room to Satan. Remember, we fight against dark spirits and demons, not against each other. We fight for one another; we pray for one another. We go to battle by prayer and by using the Bible. The scriptures are there for us to use. If we look and find verses pertaining to the situations we are facing and speak those scriptures out loud, that is power! That is us going to battle in the spirit realm. Everything happens in the spirit realm first before it affects the natural realm. Remember that! That's why the Bible says your words have power. God's Word in your mouth is *power*!

Glory to God! The Bible says our old has passed away. Our old self doesn't exist anymore, and all things have been made new. We are a new creature born of God. When Jesus died, our old self died with Him. And when Jesus arose, our new self also arose. We have become righteous! When God sees us, He sees His Son, Jesus. We must reprogram ourselves to the truth that we are not the old person any longer. The old person and behaviors will still be there, but that's where we have to start disciplining ourselves. And correct ourselves and say, "No, that is not who I am any longer." We have to speak to ourselves and remind ourselves that we are made new! And then we have the results of speaking differently and thinking differently. We will have learned not to act out but to be gentle with our responses. We will have learned how to have a quiet spirit, like God's Word asks us to have. Now all of this is done not with our own strength but with the help of the Holy Spirit. I know the task may seem impossible, but God wouldn't have said "Imitate Me" if it was. We have the ability to be and do just like Jesus. He says that we are able to do all that Jesus did, and greater things we will do. We have power! We have been given authority! We are a reflection of our Father! We are His masterpiece on display for all the world to see! We are proof of what God can do through His Children! You see, there is more to salvation than just being saved! He has called us to reign in this life. He has called us to have an excellent, successful, healthy, prosperous life! The Bible says that we are seated together with Christ in heavenly places far above! Hallelujah! We regulate our lives from a place of victory! We operate our lives from a place of rest because we know who we are in Christ! We are to enjoy the benefits of living for Jesus Christ! We can boldly declare victory after victory! If God said it, then it is so! When Jesus told His disciples to get in the boat and go to the other side, a raging storm came. The disciples had seen Jesus do miracle after miracle. They had seen Him multiply food and get money out of the mouth of a fish. They had seen Him do great things in people and heal their bodies. So when this storm came, they feared and panicked! Jesus woke up and said, "I am with you. Why did you fear? Why did you doubt?"

Time and time again, God had shown them that He was able to do the impossible! And He still shows us! He has delivered us from darkness. He has rescued us time and time again. He has set us free from strong chains of bondage. We have seen Him heal and save people, so if He has done this time after time, why would we doubt or fear in our present storm? He is with you! He is for you! He will make a way for you—always! He is mightier than the raging seas! He is the one true God! We should be confident that we will make it to the other side because He has done it for you before! You have no need to fear. You say, "I refuse to fear! I live by every word that comes from the mouth of God." It is a fight of faith! Satan wants to steal that faith from you. Satan wants you to doubt every word God has said! When he comes and whispers lies into your mind, you put him in his place! You tell him, "Devil, you have no place in my life! You have no place in my home, in my finances, in my children!" Consistently meditate on God's Word, and don't forget what you have read. You keep God's Word close to your heart. Have confidence that God is with you! He is your Shepherd. He guides you. He protects you. He watches over you and generously loves you. He said He has given you all things, so why should you need for or lack anything? He says He supplies all of your needs, so declare that! That is your truth—His Word. He has set you apart to be separate from the world. Everyone faces storms, but us believers respond differently because we know God is with us. Our results are always different than those of nonbelievers because we are not like them. We are in this world, but we are not of this world! Regulate your life from a place of peace and rest. Hold your head up high and remember who you are. You come from a lineage of miracle workers! God has made us in His image and His likeness. This means that you have been given the ability to function just like Him. He has given you the power to change any situation that comes your way. How? With your mouth. Choose to say what God's Word says concerning your situation. Refuse to allow any negative thoughts to stay planted in your mind because you will speak them. Every word you say first affects the spirit realm and then the natural realm. Your words are powerful! But God's Word in your mouth is all powerful! The Bible is alive! It has power! God gave us the Bible to use here on earth to live victoriously! Remember who you are. Remember who God is. He has unlimited supply! It is up to us to speak and declare His Word so we can possess all that He has for us. So you may enjoy all the blessings and benefits He has for you.

CHAPTER 22

God Can Turn Everything around for Good

I am in a place in my life where I am so hungry for God. I desire Him and seek to know more of Him. I live for Him and live to please Him. I am done wasting time on the wrong things. I am done allowing Satan to steal any more of my life from me. I yearn to be like Him more and more every day. The Bible says that we go from glory to glory. Line by line, precept by precept we grow, we learn, and we become transformed into that man or woman God created us to be. Go after God. Seek Him with all your heart like treasure. You will never be disappointed. The Holy Ghost inside of us gives us that ability to be like God. We have the nature of God. The Bible says, "We are no longer born of man but of God." When we receive Jesus in our hearts and make Him Lord of our life, we are no longer the "old man" but a new creation made in the image of God and given the ability to function like God. When the Bible says we are not of this world, God means it. We are to separate ourselves because we are no longer like an ordinary person. We are chosen by God—a holy nation, God's own special people!

The Bible says we are a light in this world. That we are salt to the earth. People make excuses all the time. I know, I used to be one of them. "Oh, I'm human. I'm not perfect." But why would you want to confess that about yourself? Every day, every second, every minute, we can strive to be more and more like Him.

God can trust me. God can trust the words that come out of my mouth. God can trust that I will share His Word and testify about what He has done for me. God's power flows through me when I lay hands on someone and pray. God's authority works in me when I cast out demons; they leave! God's power flows through me when I lay hands on deaf ears or blind eyes. I am sold out for Jesus! God wants to manifest His power now through all His children. He wants to do the miraculous. He wants His children to take the limits off His hands so He can do wonders, miracles, and signs! I am living the prophetic written Word of God. And He wants you to do it too. He wants to make Himself known to all. And He will do it through us! We just have to be willing to allow His power to flow. You have to give Him full access to your life so that He can do exceedingly abundantly above all you could ever ask or think.

God is real, and so is His power! I want all that God has for me. Why would any believer want just the leftovers? Take all that He has to offer. He says to have faith in Him and trust Him. God wants to manifest Himself through each of you. Read and discover the treasure inside the Bible. Allow the impurities to fall off. Let His Word correct you, pruning you to be the man or woman He created you to be. Train yourself in the gifts and anointing He has given you so that He can work through you. God's Word will transform you! Look at what He has for me. God's Word perfects us, but we must apply it to our lives. His Word transforms us. Look what He has done in my life! He transformed me. I have heard it before, "I don't want to start going to church until I stop smoking, or partying, or drinking." News flash, that day will never come. We will always make an excuse to prolong it. God says to come as you are. He already knows every mistake, every failure, and all our weaknesses. He already knows, and He loves us.

I was living the way I was living for years; it was going to take me to finally be tired of my life, be tired of what I made of my life, and surrender to God. Here I am, Lord, me and all my flaws! Little by little, things just started falling off of me. The different bad habits I had and the desire to want to do them, little by little, started to diminish. They weren't appealing to me anymore.

God's Word began to change the way I talk, the way I thought, the way I behaved, and the way I responded. His Word teaches us, builds us, leads us, and strengthens us. It is our guidebook while we live on this earth. We are only visiting this world—pilgrims. Every answer we will ever need is in the Word of God. Satan will do his best to try to keep us distracted from the things of God. Satan will put unnecessary things in our life to take up our time so we have no time for God. It is important to organize our time, organize our day so that we are able to put God first in our lives. Time is valuable these days. Everyone is always so busy that we put our things before we consider putting the things of God in our schedules. When we put the things of God first, He will add to our lives. And it doesn't just mean financially. It could be grace, or protection, or blessings. We can never lose when we serve God or put Him first. God owes no man, and we can never outgive God. He wants to lavish His blessings upon us.

There are a lot of people who say they watch church online, but it isn't the same as when you are seated in the service. Going to church is like school for believers. We too must do our own extra studying to grow more in Him. And we never stop growing. If someone in your family left a will when they passed away, wouldn't you want to know all that was left to you? Wouldn't you want to collect all that is yours? Yes! So let's find out every good and perfect thing God has for you so that you can enjoy the benefits of the inheritance He has given you. God has called all of His children to be fishers of men. He has anointed each of us to reach others for Christ. You don't have to be a preacher to save a person's life. The Holy Spirit will give you the words to say. Some people may not want to hear it; some will. Your job is to tell them, so do it. Don't you want to share what God has done in your life? Don't you want to share how He saved you? Yes, of course you do! People need to hear your story. When we share our testimony with others, we are overcoming Satan! Once you are a believer, you are no longer born of man but born of God. You are now born of the Word. We have to understand that we no longer function or speak the way a nonbeliever would because we have been reborn, recreated as a new species, a new creature. So as we read the

Bible, we apply it to our lives because we are aware of this newness within, and a retraining starts to take place from the inside out. We become more aware of who God really meant for us to be.

As you can see with my life, Satan hates me, and he hates you. He hates God. He thinks if he can keep us from God, he wins. The enemy knows what we are capable of as believers, so that is why he wants us to doubt every word. He wants us to see that a path living for God is full of rules, trying to keep us from fun. He makes us believe we can hold off salvation until later when we get older or when we are done "having fun." But tomorrow is promised to no one, so who is to say you will be able to wait? Salvation is available today for anyone. God's plan was for every man and woman to be saved. Just because God has a perfect plan predestined for each of us does not mean that it will come to pass. It is up to us to accept that path and choose to walk in that perfect plan. The devil and his demons are on a mission to destroy us all so that he can get as many of us to go to hell with him. I have met people who say they don't believe any of that stuff. Just because they don't believe does not mean it isn't true. Many are blind and deceived to the truth. Satan has scales over their eyes. Satan likes to attack us at a very early age so that he can use those hurts to affect us as we get older to destroy us. He wants to kill us, destroy us, and steal from us—steal our joy, our peace, our money, our time, and our families. He loves to attack families and divide them so children grow up broken and they then pass it on to their children. We don't have to be victims to his schemes. God already defeated Satan and all his demons! So when he shows up, we confidently tell him to go! The only power he has over your life is the permission you give him to be there. When he creeps in with depression, suicide, addiction, anger, and hate, remember who you are and remember what God has already done! Rebuke those demons in the name of Jesus, and cast them into the abyss!

God changed my life. But it didn't happen until I said yes. It is only because of Him I am able to write this book. It is only Him and the knowledge of Him that give me the ability to speak the way I do now. My life is a reflection of my heavenly Father. It is evident in my life that God is with me. I have victory after victory in my life. I have the peace of God inside me no matter what comes. His Word in me and the knowledge of His Word revealed to me have given me the confidence to stand with courage in any season. He turned my past into a story of victory. I made a decision to not become a statistic. I refused to become what people said I would be. I chose to accept what God said about me. There was a father who told his son that no matter what, people will always have something to say. He said people will always talk about you, no matter what, whether you are doing good or bad. So the father said, "Let's ride through the city, son. You on the donkey and me walking beside y'all." Sure enough, the people said how selfish the boy was for letting his poor old dad walk while he rode the donkey.

    The father said, "Okay, son, now I will ride the donkey, and you walk beside us." Before you know it, the people were saying how mean the dad was to make the little boy walk while he rode the donkey. The next day, the father said, "Now you and I both will walk alongside the donkey as we go through the city." And guess what? Yep, the people started saying how stupid they were for not utilizing the strong donkey. I shared this to show that no matter what, people are going to talk. People will discourage you from walking with God. People will ridicule you or make fun of you. But I want to encourage you to have a filter over your ears. Know that you have made the best and most important decision you will ever make. I wasted so many years on the wrong things, and now I have the opportunity to use all my strength and energy on the right things. God has turned everything around for my good, and He can do it for you too!

I am singing & sharing God's Word at an outreach in Baytown Tx.

CHAPTER 23

Get Planted in the Things of God

Have you ever received a bad grade in school? That failing grade was because you were not prepared for the tests or you just didn't understand the subject. The grade reflected how you were doing in each class. If you were doing well in school, your grades reflected that you had the knowledge being taught to you. Can you image getting a failing grade in life? Some of you may be failing now. Some of you may be doing well or barely skimming through, but what is the measuring stick you are using? If you are comparing yourself to a wealthy man who has a great wife and beautiful kids, is he really wealthy? His marriage is falling apart because he drowns himself in work to have all those nice things. So is he failing in life? If you are comparing yourself to another who also looks like their life is fantastic on social media but deals with depression and suicide every day, are they as successful as they appear? If you are comparing yourself to someone who has it all—the car, the house, the kids, the money—but is dying, are they living victoriously? We can never have a full life without Jesus Christ. We will try to accomplish and gather as much material things as we can to feel fulfilled but will always need more because nothing in this world can give us a true satisfaction like Jesus Christ. Nothing!

When we are planning to build, we first prepare the ground. Depending on the size of the building or structure, we must dig deeper than others. Not everyone's assignment here on earth is the same, so some may require digging deeper. If you are watching the progress of someone else and it discourages you, you shouldn't let it bother you. God has a special plan just for your life. You want to build your life on Jesus Christ. You want to ensure that your foundation is built on Him so you will never fall. It is called being rooted and grounded in Him so when the storms of life come, they don't move you. As a believer, you read or hear the Word. You let it get buried deep into your heart. You accept it as your truth and apply it to your life. You are building your life on Him. You are hearing His Word, and that builds up your faith. It is important to be hearing or reading the Word because it causes your faith to grow; and you begin to see miracles, signs, and wonders in your life.

The Bible says, "Now to Him who is able to do exceedingly abundantly above all you can ever ask, think or image, according to the power in you." Understand that it says "By the power in you"! God is able to do exceedingly abundantly above anything you could ever ask or image by the power in you! He has given you and me the responsibility to make those miracles happen. When you invited the Holy Spirit to come live on the inside you, He came with a power that has been given to you. God has done everything He was ever going to do. It is finished! So it is up to you to take and possess what He has given you. He says, He has given you power to get wealth, so grab ahold of it! He says, "Give attention to My Word. Give your ears to My Word, for it is health to all of your flesh!" So grab ahold of your healing. God says He is your Shepherd and makes you lie beside pleasant places, so rest in His peace. Grab ahold of His Word and begin to see your life unfold. You will have the evidence of what He says. You will see His Word working in you! Your life will be a reflection of all His goodness. People will see you and wonder why you are so peaceful going through a tough storm. People will wonder why you can be joyful during the challenges of life. It will be because of your confidence in who your God is. The Bible says that there is great reward to those whose confidence is in Him. Be sure to remain in Him. Keep your mind on Him. Keep Him first in all things. Read the Bible, then meditate on what you read all day to be sure when the challenging situations come, you are sure to open your mouth and say what God says concerning you.

The Bible says that He is perfecting all that concerns you. Isn't that amazing? How can a believer not have peace, knowing that God is working everything out for your good? You are not helpless; you are not hopeless. You have the almighty God by your side! Remember to never keep your mouth closed. Consistently confess the scriptures that you know. Stir up your spirit and ask God to give you that excitement to want to serve Him. Declare that you are addicted to His Word. Declare that your life is full of victories because it is. Believers live by faith, not by sensory perception. We don't respond by our feelings or by what we see. We speak or respond what God says. If the bills are coming in, we declare that God supplies all of our needs. A person who does not know God reacts in hate or anger. We do not because we have a gentle quiet spirit, the Bible says. If you see that you are still getting angry quickly, rebuke that demon of anger in the name of Jesus! And then we are able to respond like Jesus and walk in love. When you respond this way, you are allowing God to work in your life. And you are growing from glory to glory. And you are making progress because you hear the voice of the Lord telling you what to do. You are exactly where God wants you. You are at the right place at the right time because God is with you. You have no need to worry because His peace guards your heart and your mind. Just like now, you reading this book was an appointed time by God. He knew you were going to read this book, and He is speaking to your heart. Surround yourself with others who chose to live for God. Find a church that teaches from the Bible, a church where you can see growth and change in yourself. Keep Him first place in your life, and everything will fall into place. Remove old friends who discourage your walk with God. Sometimes it is your family members who are trying to keep you from the things of God, then you should love them from a distance until they choose to follow the Lord. Get involved with activities that help reach the lost. Make time for God. The Bible says to number our days. That means to organize our days, our hours, our minutes and be sure to have God in your day. God has such a great affection for you and desires that connection with you. As long as you are rooted and grounded in Him, you will never fail!

CHAPTER 24

Not Again

I was married to JP for five years. Our marriage from the outside looked perfect, but no one ever knows what really goes on behind closed doors. He did his best to be a good father to my daughters and accepted them as his own. He led our family in the ways of the Lord. He prayed for us and with us individually. He spoke to us about the Word. He was a good father figure to my girls. All his family loved me and my children, and mine loved him. When he wasn't out of town working, we did jail ministry at Brazoria County together, and I continued to go when he would work away from home. I was married yet was raising my daughters alone, I felt at times. I would go to work all day, come home, cook dinner, then clean or do the laundry. I was involved in church a lot. I was a praise and worship leader and had responsibilities with meetings and prayer calls while still playing the mother and wife role. During the five years of our marriage, there were conversations of me needing more affection from my husband, but it seemed like the issue was brushed under the rug. There were times my daughters would give me such a hard time when I would ask them to help clean, cut the grass, or do the dishes or laundry. Every time I had to speak to my daughters about their behavior or if they did something they weren't supposed to, I would correct them with the Word of God. Sometimes the punishment was just the disappointment I had. Sometimes it was a spanking. But sometimes I felt like *why can't they just help me? Don't they see I do everything for them?*

In the second year of our marriage, I started to get angry quickly, and I knew it was from the enemy. I would get enraged. I would go from a zero to a ten fast. I hated the way I felt inside when I would get so angry. I didn't know I could cast out the demon of rage and the demon of anger! No one taught me! Any little thing would bother me quickly, and so I remembered when Jesus was in the boat with the raging sea and said, "Peace, be still." And so when I would feel anger, I would go to the room and say, "Peace, be still," and it would go away. During our fourth year of marriage, I felt like I was pouring out all of me to everyone and everything and I wasn't getting anything back in return. I tried to have a talk with my husband again about showing me more affection, but he wouldn't. I was a beautiful woman and got compliments from strangers, but I didn't want to hear them from another man. I wanted to feel loved or desired by my husband. So in August 2015, my heart was done. I was done fighting for my marriage and not seeing a change. We separated after our fifth-year anniversary. I just couldn't see myself living the rest of my life without hugs or kisses. I was wrong. We should have sought godly counsel. But we didn't, and we got a divorce in the summer of the following year. During this separation, I stepped down from praise and worship and from jail ministry. Little by little, I started to drink. Before I knew it, I was also snorting a little coke here and there. I had told God in my jail cell in 2008 that I would never turn my back on Him, and I did. I betrayed His love and forgot about all that He delivered me from and went back to my old ways. I didn't realize that I had accepted all the lies Satan was whispering in my ear. Instead, I should have told Satan, "No, Satan, I don't hear your voice. I only hear the voice of my Father." So by me allowing Satan to persuade me, I opened the door for him to come in and destroy my life.

I continued to own and work at Studio 7, but little by little, I began to lose everything I had worked so hard for. My family was upset at me for leaving JP, but they didn't know what was going on in our marriage. Vinessa and I had packed up our belongings in a few black trash bags and left. Odessa and my son-in-law, Raymond, continued to live at our home with JP, but eventually they moved out and got their own place. I hated living out of bags. I found a trailer nearby, and we moved. My life was miserable. I knew God was missing but continued to go party. Chuye happened to be passing by my place, and he and Nano stopped. We chitchatted for a moment, and they left. I was dealing with a very mentally abusive guy I had met at the bar. He moved himself into my trailer and eventually moved his daughters in. I couldn't believe it! This guy would not go to work! He saw me struggling and chose to sleep all day and wanted to do coke all night. It was driving me crazy, and he wouldn't leave. I kept trying to get rid of him, but he always came back. Vinessa and I would take off or stay at a hotel so he could get the hint. I had wanted to go see Chuya because he had just got out of prison. For two weeks, I contemplated to go see him and finally did. Vinessa and I were on our way to Main Event, and I was going to invite him. I had on a purple blouse and my perfume—sure for him to smell. I pulled up to his mom's house in the barrio and got out to say hi. There were a lot of people there. It was kinda dark, so I couldn't make out all their faces. But he hugged me and then hugged his nieces and sister. We talked a little, and then I asked him if he wanted to go with us. He said no. His family was making him a BBQ. He didn't even know what Main Event was. I forgot he had been gone for nine years. I didn't realize what I had put Vinessa through during the separation and divorce. I was exposing her to another world she didn't know about. And she went through some depression during that time. I wasn't living for God; and I was showing her drinking was fun, partying was fun, going to the bars and playing pool was fun. I was blinded to the truth. I had allowed Satan and his demons to destroy my life and also my daughter's life. I gave him permission to come in. Not only was he killing me with depression, alcohol, and cocaine but he was attacking my baby too. Lots of times we, as parents, don't realize what is going on in our child's life because we are so wrapped up in what is going on in ours. So we don't see; we are blinded to the truth.

The following week, I invited Chuya to go eat crawfish. He said he didn't like to eat crawfish, so Vinessa and I went to eat. The following week, I took Vinessa to the rodeo carnival and posted a picture of her on one of the rides. Chuya asked on Facebook why I didn't invite him. So I called him and said, "Hey, a woman can only receive so much rejection and finally get the hint." He convinced me to pick him up after we were done at the carnival, so I did. We went to play pool and then took a drive to the beach. We started hanging around together every day—Vinessa, Chuya, and me. We would go eat, go to the movies, go to Main Event. It was fun. That guy showed up at my trailer one night when Chuya was there. He was sitting on the porch, waiting for me to get home. He didn't cause a scene because Chuya was there, and he left eventually. I moved out of that trailer and moved in with my brother Rudy for three months. Vinessa and I were back to living out of bags. I found a garage apartment for Vinessa and me, and we moved in. My life was still revolving around alcohol, and Vinessa was still battling demons of depression. I know it was because of me. Chuya would come over for dinner and sometimes stay over. I told him that I didn't want to play house, and he asked me to marry him all the while I was still working at my hair salon and still not doing too well financially. But the reason was because I spent the money as it came in. And I wasn't going to work full time. I went when I felt like it. My life on the outside looked like I was happy, but I wasn't. I ended up losing my shop due to Hurricane Harvey and because I wasn't able to pay the bills anymore. I had allowed myself to fall for every trick Satan placed in my path, and I drifted so far from God and so far from His plan for me. Four years passed, and I cried out to Him one day. My life was a mess again. I did my best to hide it, but God knew. And my spirit, the real me, knew I was living wrong. I was drinking every day and doing coke three to four times a week. The Holy Spirit would minister to me, and I knew I was missing my Father. I knew I wasn't living according to God's plan for me. I said, "God, I know You created me for something better than this! I miss You. I miss that fire I had inside for You. I miss that joy that You give, and I miss that alone time I had with You when I was in prison. I need prison, but I don't want to have to go back to prison. But I need You."

CHAPTER 25

Chuya Helped Me Open My Eyes

February 29, 2016, Chuya Montoya—fresh out the pen, full of tattoos, and big muscles. We were hanging around as friends at first but then started catching feelings for each other. We were dating for a little while when I told him I wasn't going to be playing house with anyone. That I wanted to get married eventually. I told him that if he wasn't serious about me, he should let me go.

I believe God led me to Chuya. I believe God orchestrated his release from prison just at the perfect time for me to meet him. (He has a testimony of how God did that early release for him. It was only something God would do because he had a thirty-year sentence, so he wasn't expecting to come home any time soon). I love that we were friends before. We both have a similar background and came from the same gang and hood. We fell in love, and he loved my daughters, and that is all that mattered to me.

I was not living for the Lord when I ran into him in February 2016. I was smoking cigarettes and drinking and going to the bars to shoot pool. I regret letting my daughters see me back in the world, doing what I wanted to do. Chuya and I would go out to different pool halls or karaoke bars and dances. Every weekend, we would have a new outfit to wear. We always made sure to match the color and style. We looked great together.

I would get angry sometimes; it was the insecurity of all the other relationships I had in the past, falling all on Chuya when he did nothing. I drank too much—more than I should have. I would get a party favor every now and then to even out the beer. And if I knew we were going to go out and party, there I go getting a little party snack to keep me awake longer.

My husband, Chuya, would take a video of me when we would go out only to show me the next morning. Oh, my goodness! How embarrassing. I hated to see those videos the next morning. I am naturally loud. I don't need alcohol or drugs to bring out my sparkling personality. I have it! He wouldn't take a video of me to show other people; he would do it so I could see how I acted the night before. Weekend after weekend, he would show me those videos, hoping my eyes would open. My husband wanted better for me.

Chuya helped me open my eyes to the reality of how we were living. At the same time, the Holy Spirit was calling me. He was calling me to return to my Father, but I wasn't ready. My flesh, our flesh, tries to rule us. Our flesh tries to control us and tells us what it wants. For four years, I continued to live the way I wanted to, going out drinking and partying. A lot of the parties were at our house.

As the Holy Spirit spoke to me week after week, I heard Him. I knew His voice. And I knew that I was lacking Him in my life. I knew I had no relationship with the Lord. I needed Him. I was lost without Him. I didn't have real peace. I smiled on the outside, but inside, I was broken. Although the Lord was nudging my heart, Chuya was not quite ready. He didn't want to play with God because He knew that was serious. But in actuality, God wants us to come no matter how we are or how we are living. He loves you and just wants you to come home to Him, where you belong.

At first, as I would visit a church on Sunday mornings, I would invite Chuya, but he would tell me no, he didn't want to go. It made it hard for me to want to go without him. I wanted us to grow together. Every now and again, he would go to church with me, but it was rare. I wasn't playing with God, I just knew and felt like my relationship wasn't like before. My relationship with God was nowhere near the relationship I had with Him when I was in prison. I was missing the joy I used to have. I was missing that fire I had burning inside for Him.

I cried out to God one day as I was driving. I miss You, God. I need that time with You again like I had in prison. I needed prison, but I didn't want Him to have to send me back there. I needed something to change. Then on March 31, 2019, a man ran a red light and changed my life forever. I couldn't walk. I couldn't work anymore. I needed help to go to the bathroom. I needed help to get dressed. I needed help for everyday living. I lived in pain twenty-four hours a day. I was bound to my house, like a prisoner. Like prison.

I couldn't see it at first—that this was my opportunity to get my relationship back with my Father like it was before. I didn't see the good in this situation at all. All I could see was everything I lost, everything I couldn't do, and all the places I couldn't go. I was taking a stack of pain pills daily. I was depressed because I couldn't live my life. I couldn't work anymore. How were we going to pay the bills? I couldn't walk. I couldn't go to the kitchen to grab myself something to eat while my husband was at work all day. I was helpless. So I stayed imprisoned in my bed for months and stayed in isolation because I didn't want anyone to see me. I was no longer able to go anywhere, so my husband would go and do everything alone. When I gained a little strength to move around and go places, it was so hard to get in the car and get out of the car. There was no way I could walk around the whole store, so I had to use the carts, and people would look at me badly as though I was playing on the machine, not realizing I really had a disability. I was embarrassed for my husband to have to be seen with me as I walked hunched over. My life had stopped. My body was in tremendous pain. I had good days; those were usually about a level five or six. And then I had bad days where I couldn't do anything. I had to stay lying down or sitting with my feet up. I felt like my life was over.

My husband had to come home, after working all day (labor) just to come home and cook dinner for us both. On those days, I couldn't clean, do laundry, or cook. But out of guilt, I started to work around the house because I hated the fact that I was lying around while my husband worked hard all day. So I made myself get up and do things regardless of all the pain I was in. I couldn't go anywhere or run any errands. I secluded myself that way no one could see me or know anything about me. I gained forty-five-plus pounds during my depression. I was miserable. My life was passing me by. I thought I should be out there living my life, working. I was fixing to open a new hair salon when that man hit me. When the man ran the red light, going sixty-five miles per hour, he was texting on his phone, he told the police. I remember a bright white light, and when I came to, my ears were ringing. I had no idea what had happened. A stranger ran to help me and asked me if I wanted her to contact someone. Another man came to help me to see if I was okay and advised me not to move. The lady had finally reached Chuya after two calls, and he rushed to me from Alvin. I was nearly home when this wreck happened. My daughter Vinessa would have been with me that morning, but she was away on a field trip in Louisiana with her beauty school. I had several injuries on my body, huge bruises all over my legs and feet. My back was in excruciating pain, and my legs and feet were in constant pain. I couldn't walk without help; I couldn't sit long. I couldn't stand long. I had shattered bones in my knees and bruised bone marrow. My doctor said he had never seen anything like that. After my first back surgery, the pain was so bad I thought I was going to die. I was reminded of all the pain Jesus Christ endured for me on the cross. And so I cried out, "I know the pain You endured on the cross was far worse than this, so if You could do it, I can do it too."

During the rest of 2019, Chuya and I started attending a church his parents went to. I thought it was nice for his parents to see him going to church, especially with them. All this time, I still hadn't fully given my life over to the Lord. I was still drinking, just not like before.

On December 31, we attended a New Year's church service. We had both decided we wanted our new year to have different results. We knew by us beginning the year in the house of God, changes were going to happen. And we were happy about that! Chuya started to hear the voice of God calling him. And I realized that this was my perfect opportunity to get my life back right with the Lord. I was going to use this time that I couldn't work, that I couldn't do or go anywhere to spend with God.

I finally realized that this is what I had prayed for! Solitude with my Father! So I began to read my Bible every day. I would pray and talk to God every day, just like Adam and Eve did. I relearned about all the blessings and promises that belonged to me. I relearned about the power within me. I reread all the stories about Jesus, how He spoke, and how He carried Himself; and it began to change me, little by little. I was getting stronger and stronger every day.

I was reminded about God's love for me. I was reminded about who I am and who God is and how big He is and how He has *no* limits. Little by little, my husband was going to church with me every Sunday. We stopped drinking, not because anyone forced us to but because we no longer desired it. God was starting to change our lives.

You see, I didn't belong in those places. God set me free from all of that before, and He was doing it again. I belong to God, just like you do. I belong in the house of God singing for Him, not at the karaoke bars singing all drunk. God set me free so I could share with others of His goodness, and so they could be set free too! I messed up. I turned my back on God. I opened a door for Satan to come in. But the wonderful thing about God is His grace and His mercy. He loves us and will forgive us not to purposely keep messing up but to truly want a better life—a life He can only give. To sincerely surrender our lives back to Him because we belong to Him. His tender mercy forgave me of my sins and allowed me back into His family. And you can do it too. It doesn't matter how far you have drifted away, and it doesn't matter how long you have been away from God. You can always come back. It doesn't matter what sin you have done. God Almighty loves you and wants to dwell inside you so you can be the man or woman He created you to be. God has a purpose for you, a destiny, but Satan wants to steal it from you. It is never too late to come to the feet of Jesus.

As I was being rebuilt in God's Word, I knew what the Bible said about healing. His Word says that by every stripe on His back, I am healed, not going to be healed. So that means that I believe and have faith that I am healed already, not one day going to be. Our words and our prayers first affect the spiritual world and then the natural world, which is why it is so important to watch out for the words we allow to come out of our mouths. We can either speak life or death into a situation. I choose to speak life!

Praise was also my weapon! I joined the church music team. I refused to allow the enemy or the pain to keep me from jumping and praising my God! I was alive! I realized that this accident helped me to rediscover God. The whole experience was humbling for me. My eyes started to see life differently. The scales Satan had over my eyes were falling off. Chuya and I were consistently going to church and serving God. But I remember the days he was not, and it wasn't easy. The Holy Spirit asked me, "Are you going to church for God or for your husband?" I was going to church for God. A person will have to be responsible for making his own decision whether he wants to give his life over to Jesus or not. No one can force anyone. God desires a willing heart. We have both made that personal decision to follow the Lord. And we share our testimony about how Jesus Christ changed our lives wherever we go. We recently opened a church in Alvin, Texas, called Transformation Church. We have a ministry called Building Bridges that goes out into the streets to seek the lost and get them saved! We also do jail and prison ministry. We are opening up a home called Metamorphosis Women's Transformation Home also in Alvin. We want to help people who are just like who we use to be. We go out and share what God has done in our lives to bring hope to others that if God did it for us, He can do it for them too! It is never too late!

I have learned that the enemy likes to contradict everything I am learning in the Bible. He wants me to question God. Every storm is an opportunity to learn something.

Father, what do You want me to learn from this? How can I grow from this? How can I use this storm to help myself and others? What needs to be removed from my life? Pressure and extreme heat are what form the diamond; and we, too, can utilize storms and challenges in our lives to help us be that beautiful diamond—God's masterpiece.

As I write this chapter, tears are rolling down my face because of how much my back, legs, and feet hurt right now. I know that in all things, God has a purpose. And I want Him to get the glory!

God, I want You to get the glory in my life—in every aspect of my life.

I want Him to get the glory! Every situation we go through can be an opportunity for growth in our faith because then we are able to see the hand of God at work and then share with others how He brought us out of it! I refuse to allow pain in my body to stop me from serving God. I refuse to allow Satan to steal any more of my time. I tell God, "Let me serve You strong, healthy, and whole!" I ask Him to lengthen my and my husband's days so we may complete the assignment He has given us. I want to fulfill my purpose in this life for Him. I am so grateful for my husband. I know why God placed us together. He and I are both leaders. I minister to him, and he ministers to me. We help each other. He prays for me, and I pray for him. We work as a team. He loves me, and I love him. He helps me see some situations through another perspective, and I love that about him! It is funny how God was preparing him in prison six months before his release—that he needed to change—and Chuya was obedient to the voice of God. And because he was obedient to His voice, God allowed him to be released early. He had a thirty-year sentence, and he came home in nine years! Chuya was released at the right time. God knows all things. He can turn any crooked path straight and can change the heart of any man. And because of my husband, God used him to help me open my eyes.

Chuya (Jesus) & Trudy at our wedding with my mother Rebecca and father Rudy

Chuya (Jesus) & Trudy love sharing what God has done in our lives with others

Chuye (Jesus) & Trudy we surrendered our lives over to Jesus Christ & living for God

CHAPTER 26

Rebuilding Bridges

After being released from prison in 2010, I was sent to a transition home for a short time and then paroled to my parents' house. Living on my own after all those years and then moving under my parents' roof again was challenging. I had different classes and parole visits to attend. I could not expect my parents to *stop* everything they were doing just to take me everywhere I needed to go. I had done this to myself; these were my consequences, not theirs.

I was so grateful that they would even allow me to come back home, especially after everything I put them through. But my parents opened up their home to me. They had been taking care of my girls since I started messing up my life. My dad was always working, supporting his family and supporting mine. My momma, waking up in the morning, would dress my daughters for school when it should have been me. My parents sacrificed their lives to raise my babies. I could never pay them back. We can never pay our parents back, but we can show them by making good choices, living a good life, and allowing them to see they raised us well. It was great! I was home and living with my parents and my babies.

We have to be patient with all those we hurt in the past. We can't expect them to trust us right away. Think about it. How many times did we promise it would be different, and it never was? So we have to give them time. Time to see that we are sticking to what we said we were going to do. We have to give them an opportunity to heal, just like we did.

Be helpful when you get home. Help around the house, cook, maybe clean, cut the grass, or look for a job. Learn to listen and hear what it is they are saying or trying to say. We have to show them with our actions that we will do every word we said. So have patience with yourself as well.

Before, when I would get out of jail, I would create a list of ten things to do when I got out. Things like getting a job, buying a car, going to school, getting a license—all of these are great goals, but we can't put too much on ourselves. And it was so overwhelming because when I would look at all these things on my list, I couldn't do them all at once. So I would give up and quit and fall into that same pattern every time. But this time, I only put three things on my list. I accomplished them one at a time, and it felt amazing! And then I would add another goal.

Maybe you can do the same and create a short list of things you want to do or need to do. And once you accomplish that list, add another goal until you have achieved them all!

Living back under my parents' roof was such a challenge for me because there were a lot of hidden issues that never were resolved between my mom and myself. All the past anger and unforgiveness toward her, I forgave, but we never spoke about it. I think we should have talked about it. It would have helped me heal—I think. But just because I forgave her didn't mean she had changed. And when I moved back in, I was experiencing everything all over again like all the times before. I didn't like seeing or hearing the way she treated my dad. I didn't like the way she wanted to be in control of everything. I didn't like that she picked on everything I did. I didn't like the way she spoke to me or my daughters. Everything I did was never good enough for her. I didn't like her character. And so we would bump heads a whole lot as I was growing up. But as an adult and as a follower of Jesus Christ, I didn't want her behavior or ways to bother me. So, instead, I would go pray because God had truly changed me and because before I would argue back with her. I wouldn't let her get away with telling me anything; I would defend myself. But I didn't want to respond that way anymore. I wanted peace in my life, so after eight months of living under their roof, I moved out. I wasn't able to take my daughters with me because they had temporary custody over them. And I still needed to show them I had changed. Sometimes my mom would tell me that I wasn't going to get my daughters back. But I would go fight on my knees, reminding God and myself of what His Word said. My dad did everything for my mom. He loved her and agreed with everything she said. My dad would have the final say in some matters, but she was the boss. She didn't like anyone telling her anything. My brothers, my daughters, and I grew up watching a woman dominate the home and her man. She loved to control. I don't want to portray my mother in any of her bad behaviors. I never wanted or want to be like my mom. I wanted to be better and different than her. I loved my daddy, but it was as though she stole that daddy-daughter relationship because he always chose her side when she and I would disagree. The one time I tried to speak up for him, he slapped me. And I told myself I would never defend him again. But I should have! I should have spoken up for him. But he loved her. He chose her, and he knew the way she was and continued to stay with her.

    If you have a difficult situation with someone, pray. Don't fight physically or verbally. After giving my life to God, I was able to walk away and go pray in another room. As I would walk away, I would cry because of the old me, because the words said would hurt me so bad, and because the old me wanted to jump out of me, but I had already disciplined myself not to respond like that anymore. I was a new person. And I was going to fight on my knees in prayer. I want to advise you to do the same. Don't allow someone else's character or actions to destroy you. You cannot change anyone but yourself. While I was in prison, I had already surrendered all my past hurts to Him, and He healed my heart. So the best thing for me to do was love from a distance, even if it meant staying away from my daddy, which hurt me because I wanted to keep my relationship with him. But there was no way to see him without her tagging along. So my visits to see them were short because she would either start some negative talk with me or with him, and so I would leave. But I want to encourage you to mend the bridges that you broke. Allow God to fix them. Invite Him into the situation. Your job is to walk in love, and if they don't accept that, then love them from a distance and pray for them that one day their eyes will be opened to the truth. Recently, I had an opportunity to speak to my mother. I prayed first that every word spoken would come from the Holy Spirit and that she would receive them with love. I was able to tell her how her words and actions used to hurt me. I told her that I forgave her and that I loved her. The Lord had led me to start a weekly Bible study in January 2022. In the beginning, Emmanuel Worship Center allowed us to hold the studies there, which I am so grateful for. Then later, the owners of Alvin Wellborne Cinema, Andrew and Janie, would allow us to use their theater to hold these Bible studies. Sometimes we would rent out hotel conferences. There was just an urgency God placed in my spirit to have them. My mom would attend each week, hearing and listening to the Word of God. And I started to see progress in her life. I could see a change in her character. I knew God was working in her life and that God was rebuilding that bridge that was once broken between me and her. God is restoring our relationship! God is healing our relationship. In all the tough seasons, God wants to get the glory in it! God wants us to have a testimony. And He's got the glory in this. My mother is trying to change. My mother is seeing the areas in her life that need to change. And she repented. She is allowing God's Word to change her from the inside out. And now we are able to talk and laugh. I am able to hug her and show her love. And she is able to be involved in my life like she always wanted to. And God can do the same for you! Isn't that amazing? God can bring to life the dead! God has also given me the opportunity to love and forgive Diablo and his wife. Satan tried to bring so much turmoil and division. So much pain, anger, unforgiveness, and rejection, but God received all the glory in the end! God erased and healed the past. He brought rejoicing and singing. He brought unity and forgiveness. God mended all my broken bridges. He can restore our lives better than before! All we have to do is let Him. He can repair and rebuild our lives! His mercy, His grace, and His love are so awesome!

CHAPTER 27

The Beginning of Building Bridges Ministry

I have been arrested over twenty-six times. Every year, I was locked up for nine months, six months, two weeks, and three weeks. It would never fail. Brazoria County Jail was my second home. Year after year, it was the same thing; I was the one missing at all my family gatherings. I already knew once I was released that it wouldn't be too long until I was back again. I would tag my issued clothes with "Troop" or the dog paw for the Barrio Dogs gang I was in. All the guards knew me. When I would get locked up, I would request a black Holy Bible. I would also attend the church services. I would highlight scriptures I knew and wrote letters home saying, "This time it would be different." In my heart, I really wanted it for me. I knew my spirit was crying out for help. One minute, I wanted to do right; and the next minute, I was fighting a demon of addiction. I was addicted to the lifestyle as well. When I would sell drugs, people always needed me. But in actuality, they didn't need me; they needed the dope I had. In December 2007, the judge was so tired of seeing me in and out of his courtroom that he told me, "If I see you one more time, I'm giving you ten years." I said, "Yes, sir!" Then two months later, the laws had caught me again. After requesting to be put in solitary—two months of solitude—a chaplain gave me a devotional. When I read an article in there, I discovered it was God who was missing from my life. I got on my knees and asked for forgiveness. I asked Him to be Lord of my life. Once the guards placed me back into population where all the other inmates were, it was different for me. It wasn't like all the other times I had gotten locked up. Normally, I was the one telling the nasty jokes and making the best out of being locked up. However, this time, I was really washed clean of my sins. I had really given my life to the Lord. So that was when I started my ministry. I didn't have a name for it yet because I didn't know it had begun. I would talk to the girls in there about what I was reading in the Bible that day.

Some wanted to hear, some didn't, which is cool because they weren't ready. I would read my Bible every day instead of playing cards or watching TV. I wasn't doing my jail time that way this time. I was serious about my new decision to give Jesus my life. As I would read, I could hear God's voice, telling me it was time to give up cussing. I could be talking to someone about Jesus one minute and cussing crazy the next.

God spoke to me. He said that freshwater and saltwater do not come out of the same faucet. *Wow*! That was exactly what I had been doing. Blessing and cursing coming out of the same outlet. So I made a decision not to cuss anymore. I was going to slap myself until I stopped. For three days, I slapped myself. They would ask, "Nunez, why are you slapping yourself?"

I said, "I don't want to cuss anymore." And with a little discipline, I stopped. Again, this is what it took for me.

I would study every day, digging my roots down deep. I knew that I needed to get strong in the Lord because all those things that caused me to get locked up were going to try to pull me back in once I was released. Every day, my Lord would speak to me. He was changing me from the inside out. There were challenges I faced in prison, but nothing I couldn't handle.

I was allowing God's Word to change my life. When we behave opposite of what God's Word says we are, we are behaving out of character. I knew that when we are lost without Christ, anything goes. Sin! The enemy loves to twist up everything good that God creates. He loves to pervert it. So the enemy knew that I had feelings for girls, so he tried to use that in there with me.

I overcame those thoughts; I overcame those feelings. I found a verse in the Bible, in Romans, that says, to see young girls as your sisters and see older women as your mothers. So I allowed God's Word to start affecting that part of my life. And it's gone. He removed the desire of lust over women. He removed the perversion of attraction to women.

He has done that for me with alcohol too. He just took it way. I don't even think about it. It's called being free. God started changing me little by little. The changes didn't happen overnight. I had been living the way I wanted to for so long; the change would take some time. And God knew. I would find a Scripture, and the Holy Spirit would speak to my heart, and then I would want to change that about myself.

God's Word changed the way I spoke and the way I thought. His Word taught me to think first before responding, not reacting. I would consider first, "What will happen if I do this, or if I say that?" I never used to think that way. I would do whatever I wanted whenever I wanted. I had no self-control. I had no discipline. I am so thankful to God for changing my life!

I used to be a remote control. If someone pushed my buttons wrong, I would react! If something made me mad, I would just react with words or physically. That is not a way to live. We should always stop and think first. God's Word taught me to have a quiet, gentle spirit. It brought peace to my life.

I would speak to the different girls who were in my dorms. I would minister to them. I would give godly counsel. I would pray over them when they would ask. I didn't waste my time watching television. I didn't play cards. I drew a picture for every story in the Bible. I wrote many songs. I journaled every day and just studied the Bible. I pretended prison was like Bible camp, a strict one. And this is where God placed it in my heart to help other women like me. Help women who are ready for change. The women's home we are opening will be a strict six- to nine-month program. They will study the Word of God and pray. They will allow God in so He may heal them of all their past hurts and disappointments. They will have a gym so they may receive physical healing as well. There will be a garden so they will experience what I did with God as I worked in the fields in TDC. If they don't have their GED, we will help them obtain it. We will also ensure that they have employment and housing before they graduate. I want to help women get out of the endless cycle. I want to give them another option than being a statistic. Metamorphosis is located in Alvin, Texas. If you or someone you know is ready for change, please contact us. We want to help women like me.

Building Bridges Ministry–Trudy singing with an anointing of the Holy Spirit touching lives to never be the same again

CHAPTER 28

God's Perfect Timing

Once I was transferred out of Brazoria County, they sent me to Plane State to serve for eighteen months. Mind you, this was my first time in prison. I was used to intake at the county jail but never at a prison unit. The guards unloaded all of us out the van and brought us inside. All the inmates getting checked in had to stand up against the wall and disrobe. The room was not private. There were inmates all around you—some getting checked in themselves from other counties. We had to spread our legs and bend over while people were looking at you naked. But these were the consequences of all of our actions. Once we went through that humiliation, we had to take a quick shower and put powder on our hair for lice prevention. We had to take our picture for our prison ID and get the necessary blood work needed and assessment. They gave us all a shot in the arm to determine if we had TB. Once diagnostic was done, they assigned us to our dorm and bunk. I arrived in the summer, so it was hot. Sometimes, I felt as though we were all cattle in those dorms. It would get so hot that I would shower and not have to dry myself afterward because by the time I got back to my bunk, I would be dry. Each inmate was assigned a job on the unit; no one was able to sit around all day unless you had bad medical issues. My first job on that unit was shipping and receiving. We loaded and unloaded trucks that came in. We would organize everything that came into the unit. We were the ones in charge of distributing toilet paper or whatever was needed, either in the dorms or offices. I really enjoyed that job. One day, they assigned me to the kitchen. There, we were responsible for the meals everyone would eat. We had to wash all the pans and clean up the chow hall afterward. One morning, after everyone ate, it was time to clean the chow hall. I was getting my mop bucket ready to mop. I looked up, and everyone was gone. The other girls were hiding, not wanting to help clean. God spoke to me. He said, "Not everyone is going to be excited about doing ministry with you. There will be times you will go alone. Not everyone is going to want to serve Me, like you. So don't be discouraged. I am with you."

Every day in prison, God spoke to me. He ministered to my spirit. I *loved* prison! I am so glad that I went. I needed it! Every day, God removed things from my heart. He was changing me into the woman He created me to be.

When I first started working, I knew I was going to need a clock to wake me up each day. There was no one to tell you "Wake up, you are going to be late for work." And if you were late, you would get a write-up. Those write-ups can add more time to your sentence. I wasn't going to be able to go to commissary for a while to buy one. And there I was reminded of how God always brought the sun out on time. God always sent the moon back on time. And so I asked Him if He could do the same for me until I could buy a clock. And He did! He would wake me up every morning at the same time on time. God is truly amazing, and all He wants is to be a part of our lives.

Parole had come to see me. They asked me questions, and I answered. They denied me leaving early. I was a little upset about that but was reminded that I had asked God not to let me leave prison until He said I was ready. There was clearly more for me to learn. And I thanked God I didn't leave because that evening, a young girl, not even eighteen yet, was going to serve many years. I started to minister to her in Spanish. The Holy Spirit was giving me the words to say. She understood everything. She was ready to receive Jesus into her heart. And she did.

I have been cutting and coloring hair since I was in my early teens. I had made a habit of just cutting all my hair off when I was sad, angry, or depressed throughout my life. I didn't know why it would make me feel better afterward. And so when I would get locked up, I would cut mine or the inmate's hair. I had gotten really good at shaving with the razor and fading with the fingernail clippers. During my time in Plane State, I had asked God to help me find a career for when I got out. I had such a long record; it was hard for me to find a job that would hire me. That was another reason why I would always go back to selling dope. No one would give me a chance. But I didn't want to make that same mistake again, so I sought God to show me what I needed to do to financially support my daughters and myself. And one day, it dawned on me. I was going to go to school to do hair. I would tell the girls in there, "When I get out, I'm going to open up my own shop and put an LED light of fingernail clippers instead of scissors." They would laugh.

I remember asking God to please help me learn how to dress like a momma. I had always worn Dickies. I could wear any style really. But I wanted God to begin to change my outside too. It's tough for someone like me. People want to look at my tattooed arms first before they get to know the real me.

I would pray, "Father, I want my daughters to be proud of me. Let me be an example to them where they imitate me imitating You." God has always been so patient with me. So forgiving, so loving. He has always been there for me even when I wasn't aware of it. I remember this man saw me walking the streets of Houston with nowhere to go. It was cold, and I hadn't eaten. He pulled up next to me in a wrecker truck. He asked me if I was hungry. He had a whole Thanksgiving feast at his house and invited me to join him and his family.

(Pause) God sent a stranger to invite me into his home. I'm sure I wasn't dressed for the occasion, but they all accepted me with open arms. I ate and asked him to drop me back off.

God knows our beginning and our end. In spite of all of my mistakes, my life choices, and all the tragedy I went through, none of it was in vain. God uses all of those situations for me to encourage others who might be going through the same thing. The devil wanted to kill me in my sin. He tried to destroy my life—my future and my children's lives. He tried. But he lost! Sin will take us further than we want to go. Sin will cost us more than we want to pay. Sin will keep us longer than we want to stay. But God saw something in me I couldn't see myself.

CHAPTER 29

At the Right Place at the Right Time

After my eighteen months in Plane State, I was transferred to a unit in Huntsville. Now in this unit, I was assigned to work in the fields. If you have drug charges, you are automatically assigned to the Hoe Squad. Each inmate is lined up in a straight line with hoses in our hands. We have to swing those bad boys high, and if not, you get a write-up. You don't want write-ups because they can hinder an inmate from going home on time. I loved it, though, working outside in the sun. I had to rebuild my strength especially to keep up with the other girls, so I would do curls with bags of bottled waters. I was determined to work just as hard as everyone else.

Planting, pulling out weeds, watering, and picking the vegetables. God spoke to me a whole lot while I would be out there in the sun. We handpicked a whole field; it was awesome. I wouldn't trade my days in prison for anything. He would speak to me about removing weeds from my own life. We have to, or those weeds kill us and hinder us from growing spiritually. All this time in prison, He was just changing me every day. And I loved it! I loved my alone time with Him.

He is so awesome. The sunsets and sunrises were so glorious out there in Huntsville. The girls there knew that my fruits were evident and that I was truly living for Jesus Christ. They would ask me for advice or for prayer.

Every two weeks, my dad and mom would send me twenty-five dollars for commissary. Wow! They really shouldn't have done it, because I was the one who was responsible for putting myself there. But that's the love my parents had for me; they made sure I was taken care of. They sent me money to buy extra food, snacks, or clothing and shoes. They didn't have to, but they loved me regardless of where I was and of what I had done. They wanted me to get my life together.

My dad supported me and my daughters when he didn't have to. He had his own bills to pay. He and Mom raised their children, and here they were, raising mine. My mom and dad made sure to bring my girls to come and visit me every three weeks. Whether it was in Plane State Penitentiary, or the prison units in Huntsville, Texas, they would come. It wasn't a thirty-minute drive either. Daddy would make sure to bring his pockets full of quarters so my daughters could buy snacks for them and me. My momma made sure to write me a letter every week. Every week! Just to catch me up on everything that was going on so I wouldn't feel left out. She would send me photos all the time to make sure I could see everything and everyone at the get-togethers. She would encourage me with those letters. She would tell me one day that I would wake up and it would all be like a dream. She would write me and tell me that I would be home soon and that they were waiting for me.

One day, we were all in line for chow. I was in Huntsville at this time. My arms were toward my back. My wrist was resting in my other hand. My hand was cupped open. We all had to walk around the unit with our hands behind our backs. A small three-inch branch fell into my hand. How could it be? My hands were practically closed. I don't know how that little stick made it into my hand. I looked up and told God, "You know exactly where I am. It is not a surprise to You." He let me know I wasn't alone.

The prison units have yellow-sprayed lines everywhere. We, the inmates, are supposed to follow them everywhere we walk. Some girls would cut the corners, trying to get where they were going a little faster. I wouldn't. They would ask, "Nunez, why don't you just follow us and cut the corners? You don't have to follow the lines perfectly." I told them, "I don't want to. If I can't follow the rules in here, I'm not going to follow them when I get out."

I would really enjoy the men and women volunteer chaplains who would come to lead the church services or would teach classes. I would always cry, not out of guilt or shame but because I was finally free! God had set me free. And I was really happy, not because of things but because of what God was doing in my life.

I remember, a man of God, Eddie B, came to preach and sing at our unit. During his service, I knew right then what I wanted to do when I got out. I wanted to do jail and prison ministry. I wanted to come back to the places God brought me out of and share with other convicts like me that if God could change someone like me, He could change them too.

So out of my eighteen months State and three years TDC, I did one month and a half shy of two years total. Yeah! I remember about six months prior that I had told God, "I know that I asked You not to let me leave prison until You said I was ready. But I am ready to go home." And He let me. I was back home with my babies!

I wrote many songs in prison. "Secret Place," "Rain Down on Me," "I Want to Grow," and "Break Free" to name a few songs, I was able to sing in a few cities in Texas. Different churches, Christian groups, women's homes and rehabs would give us an opportunity to come to play and sing and share my testimony. We had a band called Dayz of Mercy. My brother Gabriel and Odessa were in it. A few other guys, too, played the guitars and drums. Gabriel played the keyboard and sang, and Odessa sang as well.

When I sing, I pray for people to feel God penetrating their hearts. I pray that when I speak, His Word pierces their spirit. That healing and salvation take place when they hear my voice. I pray that chains are broken, and people are set free when they hear my songs and voice. I sing for the honor and the glory of the Lord. I owe Him everything. He has done so much for me. I owe God my life. And I give it to Him gladly. I am a vessel of honor for Him. I serve Him and adore Him. I love getting on my knees and praying to Him or just bowing to Him to show Him my adoration toward Him. "Use me, Lord!" I pray my songs are heard one day. We opened a place of worship called Transformation Church. I want to spread the Gospel to my nation, to my city, and to my friends and family. I am on fire for God! And He has surrounded me with laborers who are on fire as well and are ready to serve.

Building Bridges Ministry–Trudy going out into the streets of Houston Tx. Leading people to Jesus Christ & setting them free

CHAPTER 30

When Will You Make That Decision?

The *best* decision I ever made in my life was asking Jesus Christ to be the Lord of my life. His eyes have been on me before I was in my mother's womb. He knew every choice I would ever make. He knew every mistake and every achievement. He knows my strengths and my weaknesses. He knows me inside out. And He still chose to die for me so that one day, I will be with Him for all eternity. He never once turned His back on me even when I chose to do it to Him. He loves me so much—all of us really!

I love to get on my knees to pray to Him and worship Him. I thank Him. I have so much to be thankful for. I tell Him how awesome and wonderful He is. There was no god before Him, and there will be no god after Him. He is the one true God. He is alive and powerful!

The Bible says that we each are responsible for our own salvation. We must work out our own salvation. No one can do it for you or me. We have to accept what Jesus did. Receive Him in our hearts. And it is up to us to study and read on our own. Our pastors at church can only teach so much; we too must have that alone time with God so He can grow us into the person we were created to be.

Actively pursue God. Desiring on our own to grow in our relationship with Him. During that private time, He speaks to us. He answers us and our intimacy with Him grows. Our eyes begin to see the truth. And our perception of life changes. It is a beautiful thing.

Every day, I desire for others to have that walk with the Lord. I, too, was lost and know what it is like to live a life without Him. Don't wait; we are not promised tomorrow.

God has set me free. He has given me a new life by forgiving me. And now I have a life I can be proud of

CHAPTER 31

God Can Give Us a Supernatural Peace

I lost six family members during the year 2020. My father, Rudy Nunez Sr., passed away on December 18, 2020. That was a devastating time in my life. My husband, too, lost his father, Jaime Montoya Sr., six months before. I don't believe time heals our pain, but it's Jesus Christ who heals the brokenhearted. Our fathers were taken early; they were still young.

They were both cheerful men who loved their families and worked hard to support them. I believe we keep a person alive by sharing stories of their lives with our children and grandchildren. We keep them alive by remembering what they wanted you to do or be in life.

The Holy Spirit rose up inside me and said I would take the lead. I would carry on the thing my father loved—Jesus. I would allow God to use me more than He did with my dad. Every blessing and prayer my dad requested, I asked God to pass it on to me. They belonged to me. I was going to carry on the name of Jesus! I was going to minister to my children, my grandchildren, my family, and my friends any opportunity the Lord gave me.

That season was challenging. Learning to live without my daddy was going to be difficult. I was going to have to learn how to live without him. I was not going to pick up the phone and call him or go see him whenever I wanted. I wasn't going to be able to run and sit on his lap anymore. There was going to be a void or emptiness, not only in my heart but also in the room during our family get-togethers.

I have asked God to surround me with His peace and comfort. I know that my daddy is in glory. And when Jesus returns, I will go and meet my dad in heaven. Grieving is different for everyone. Everyone deals with grief or the loss of a loved one differently. Some people take longer to feel happy again or even willing to move on. But we must be careful because it could be an opportunity for Satan to come in with depression.

I regret not spending more time with my dad. I regret not sitting on his lap as much as I really wanted to. I regret not being able to see him anymore. We go to his gravesite and catch him up on things that are happening, but I know he isn't there. Love your parents. Spend time with them. Tell them thank-you. Smell them and kiss them. It was hard going into my parents' room, Odessa, Vinessa, my brothers Rudy and Gabriel, and my mom, looking at all my dad's things. We were remembering when he wore that piece of clothing or what he had said about this gun or when he wore that particular cap. My daddy loved pens, guns, fishing, and caps, and he loved the Lord.

I was so happy that my daddy got to see me changed. I was so happy my dad got to see me serve the Lord and live for God. Each of my family members handled his death in their own way. I know, I would never blame God for my daddy's death. We live in a dark world. Bad, tragic things happen to everyone. This world is ruled by darkness. COVID took my daddy.

We all prayed for healing for him. We all thought he was coming home. Because of the COVID outbreak all around the world, they did not allow us to go into the hospital to see my daddy. Not once did we get to go in and visit him. He stayed in that hospital room alone. No family to hold his hand. The nurses and doctors said he couldn't breathe without the help of the oxygen mask, so we didn't call too much; we didn't want to hurt him or make him talk more than he had to.

We would call his room, and we would all pray with him. We would encourage him and, of course, tell him we loved him, that he wasn't fighting alone, we were all fighting with him, and that we were all waiting for him. The nurses really never gave a true explanation of the severity of my dad. We thought he would be home in three days. After a few days of the regular breathing tube through the nose, it wasn't enough for him, and they said they were going to have to put him in the ICU. A week before, the Holy Spirit spoke to my heart, encouraging me to get my family to video call him early in the morning and pray with him. So we did just that. Little did we know what was to come.

I guess we didn't understand he would be unconscious in the ICU. And still, they made us feel as though he was good and he would be coming home soon. As the days went by, we were not able to talk to him at all. They had a tube down his throat. All the status updates would sound great, then some wouldn't sound too good. We thought he was coming home.

We received a call, asking us to make a difficult decision. How could this be? Making a decision to turn off the very machine that was keeping my daddy alive. How? We didn't want to let him go!

Once we determined to unplug the machine, then the hospital said we could come and say our goodbyes. I wish we could have done that while he was awake. Now we would have to go into the cold hospital room and see our daddy sedated. We were told to dress up in hospital gear to ensure our safety. But my dad was covid-free. So we couldn't kiss him because of the huge plastic masks they made us wear. We held his hands and rubbed his feet. We kept calling his name and telling him, "Daddy, we love you." I turned on some Christian music and was praising the Lord as my family hovered over my daddy's body. My momma was talking to my dad, and he responded, "Yeah," that he could hear us. Man, we were all crying in disbelief. Sadness filled that room. My little brother looked at me with such a broken heart. We were all heartbroken.

How are you supposed to go on from the death of someone you love? Call on Jesus. Do not carry this burden alone. He wants us to throw onto Him everything that troubles us. He wants us to live in peace with no worry or concern. Those burdens are not for us to carry. I know it's hard. You may think you are not loving that person who passed if you are not grieving, but that's not true. Of course, you love them, but God will give a way to live peaceably through it. Some days are tough, but somehow God removes the hurt and gives me comfort. I know that my heavenly Father loves me so much He doesn't want me to stay in the sadness. And He will be there for you too if you let Him. He will reach into the dark hole you are in and pull you out and give you an unexplainable peace.

Gabriel, Trudy, Rebecca, Rudy Sr., Rudy Jr.

My Daddy Rudy Nuñez Sr praying over a man

CHAPTER 32

Without Faith, It Is Impossible to Please God

January 2021, Chuya and I made a decision to try IVF. I stopped taking all my pain medication in October 2020, so my system could be clean. It was exciting traveling, getting to know each other more, and seeing what these doctors could actually do. We signed up for a program they had: four IVF treatments, and if they didn't get me pregnant, we get that initial money back. That didn't include expenses for the medication, the hotel, the plane tickets, and the food. So we left for Monterrey.

For our first IV treatment, we did everything right, medication and appointments; the retrieval and the transfer were a success. We flew back home and waited. After the fourteenth day, it was obvious the transfer didn't take. All my at-home pregnancy tests were coming back negative. I didn't feel too healthy mentally or physically; my dad had just passed away. I was pretty emotional about it not working. All I could do was cry. I decided I was going to open the Bible and start reading in Deuteronomy about the blessing that belongs to me.

Before we could return to Monterrey for our second IVF treatment, we had to wait for two cycles to pass. The doctor said it was better. So we waited. But during that waiting time, I continued to read the Word of God. I was building my faith in the Lord. I also made sure to eat better and more, preparing my body for a little baby to live inside me. Once the two cycles passed, it was March, and we left back to Monterrey. I had to take hormone shots in my belly, and they hurt. I had to take daily shots and medication to prepare my body and womb for pregnancy. After the transfer, we came back to Texas to wait for fourteen days. All my pregnancy tests were coming back negative. The transfer was not successful again. Ugh. I knew what God's Word said. It said no barren among me. I knew the words of prophecy spoken over me—that God would give me the strength to carry my child and still do all He called me to do. I knew the written Word that pertained to me! I knew the blessings and promises that belonged to me.

So during the waiting, I stayed in God's Word and continued to pray. We set a schedule for our third IVF treatment for May. We were pros already. We knew how to get around the airport; we knew where to park. Everything was easier. The shots and medication schedule was easier, and we had high hopes we would leave Mexico pregnant!

In 2000, after delivering Vinessa, the doctor asked about tying my tubes, I said, "No, I would like something temporary because I still wanted to have a little boy." Little did I know, the doctor had cut and burned my tubes. When I found out what he had done, too much time had passed. I wouldn't be able to do anything about it through the doctor. I wanted to have a baby boy after having Odessa and Vinessa. I wanted to have three to five children. Of course, in all of my twenties, I am so glad I didn't get pregnant while I was out there living in chaos. God puts that desire of wanting a family in us. He calls us to be fruitful and multiply. The Bible says that children are a heritage from God, and the fruit of the womb is a reward.

I spent years hoping and anticipating a baby. Every month, I would faithfully, pray, and pray for a baby. I would make sure to go to the front of the church every time they called out to someone wanting to have a baby. I felt if I could just get someone to pray over me, the baby would come. I would pray and confess that I would get pregnant and have a baby. I would beg and cry out to God to please, please, please give me a baby. Ugh, it was such an emotional rollercoaster. Once my period would come, I would get so sad and lose my faith. It was so very heartbreaking.

Month after month, I would question myself, *What was I doing wrong? Was my faith not real or strong enough? Was I praying wrong?*

Was I doing something wrong? I would pray for God to restore my eggs. Oh, I wanted to have a baby boy so bad.

Chuya doesn't have any children. He wants to be a daddy. I know he has my daughters to love, but they are grown, and it isn't the same. We wanted a baby or two from our genes—together. A child that looks like him and me. The Bible says that our children are like olive plants all around our table.

I am forty-five years old, and the world says that I am too old to have babies. My tubes are burned and cut, so they say I can't have children. But God's Word says I can! And I believe what He says. Let it be unto me what His Word says. That's what faith is. And the Bible says, "Blessed is the one whose trust is in the Lord." I live by what God's Word says, not people. God has the final say. And nothing can stop the works of His hand. There is no limit to God. He loves to get the credit for miracles! And I love for Him to get the glory in my life. I believe my husband and I will be pregnant by the hands of the Lord. When I speak His Word, over any situation, His Word does not come back void.

Today I understand that my old perception was wrong. Also, wavering faith was not good. Having faith all month to lose hope or question God when my cycle would come is not faith. James 1:6 says, "But let him ask in faith, with no doubting, for he who doubts is like a wave of the sea driven and tossed by the wind." Plus, I am to live and walk by faith, not by what I see. Our faith pleases God and causes His power to move on our behalf.

If God did it for someone else, He will do it for me too! That is why I love hearing people's testimonies of how God impregnated them with a miracle baby. Our God is big and is able to show us great and mighty things! So my husband of three years, Chuya, and I decided to do IVF. Plus they had a money-back guarantee.

We got back to Texas after our third try and waited. The anticipation was high! By the fifth day, I was feeling nauseated! It was great! I knew I was pregnant! The doctors had transferred two baby embryos into my belly. Oh, what joy! We were so excited! Twins—we were going to have twins. I was considered high risk because of my age and because we were having twins. Everything was going great until one doctor visit. I was feeling uncomfortable.

As I was driving, I was having pains in my lower abdomen. I signed myself in at the clinic and had a seat. I got up to go use the restroom and a gush of pink water come out of me. I was freaking out because I didn't want to lose my babies. I got cleaned up and went to a private room. I was explaining everything to the doctor. They were requesting for me to see a high-risk doctor so I could be under his care. As I drove home, I had the urge to use the restroom. I pulled into a store and parked. Before I could get out of the truck all the way, a gush of something came out of me. I rushed to the restroom as safely and quickly as possible.

As soon as I sat down on the toilet, I cupped my hand under me, and gush, a lot of blood, and a sac with two babies inside smaller than my hands came out. I just held them and wept. I had just lost my twin babies. I phoned my husband, and he rushed to meet me. We took off to the emergency room in Clear Lake. They ran a lot of tests and took blood from me as well. The blood they took from me was still showing I was pregnant. One nurse also gave me hope that she, too, lost a huge amount of tissue before, and her child was grown.

A week later, the next doctor's visit confirmed I had a miscarriage. I was so heartbroken. I didn't understand how that could happen. All I could do was cry. My cycle didn't come as scheduled. I felt nauseated like when I was pregnant a month ago. Nah, I couldn't be! I went and bought three tests! All three of them were showing pregnant. What? This was all God. I got pregnant with no doctors and no medication. It was a miracle! I was telling everyone everywhere I went how God got us pregnant all by Himself. What a testimony!

Three weeks later, I lost that baby too. It was sad. I was confused. How could this happen? God showed us that He could get us pregnant. He didn't need help. I continued to stay in the Word, reading and praying. Both of our faith had grown. We both knew that God is faithful, especially to His Word. Two months later, we scheduled for our fourth IVF treatment. We really didn't want to go back. Our heart wasn't in it like before. We had already seen God do it on His own. So when we got back to Texas, we waited for fourteen days. All my tests were coming back negative. We didn't get pregnant. Instead of being depressed and angry, we rejoiced and praised God regardless of what the situation looked like.

I asked God, "Did I do what Sarah did, like in the Bible?" Sarah was trying to help God out. Or she thought God was taking too long. So she let her man sleep with another woman so they could have a baby. Was I trying to make God move quicker?

God told me, "Don't focus on what didn't happen in Mexico. Focus on the lives you touched, prayed over, and changed while you were in Mexico." Here, I was feeling horrible about losing my babies, and the money, the time, and all our efforts to come back empty-handed; but in reality, we made a difference when we were in Monterrey.

I believe what the Bible says about me and having more children. He showed me a verse in September 2021: "I am The Creator, who formed you and the world. I am the One True God. I call you by name. No one can stop the work of my hands. I can make a way. I can make paths in the raging seas. Do not think about the former times. Do not consider the days of old. For I am doing a new thing and it will surely come to pass. I make roads in the wilderness and rivers in the desert."

God said to my spirit, "Trudy, do you think I need help getting you pregnant? Do you think I need help? Do not remember all the other times it didn't work. Don't even consider your age. Trudy, I am doing a new thing, and it will surely come to pass."

IT'S NEVER TOO LATE

Chuya (Jesus) & Trudy in Monterey Mexico going through IVF Treatments

CHAPTER 33

It's Never Too Late with God

My story isn't over. I will sing to the Lord until He calls me home. I will serve my God wherever I go until the day I die. I will continue to do outreaches and serve at places I'm invited to. At this time, Brazoria County has put a pause on church services, so until they let me back in, meanwhile, I attend Stringfellow Prison Unit. I love sharing with others what God is doing in my life. Remember, any situation you go through can bring God glory. You can share with others what happened and how God turned it around. Everything you go through is not in vain. You can encourage someone not to give up. Life isn't over; it is just beginning.

It is *never* too late with God. God's Word can turn the heart of any man or woman. You may be on a path right now where you think it's the end of your life, but you are *wrong*! If you give your heart to Jesus, it will be the beginning of a new life. Prisoner, homeless, drug addict, alcoholic, gambler, prostitute—whatever it is, God can turn it all around. Things will start falling into place because you will be on the right path. God's favor would follow you everywhere you go. The Lord wants to set you free so that you can have true liberation. There is *nothing* like the peace of God in your spirit. I pray as you read this book you will be transformed.

God wants to take you to a new level of life of faith. The atmosphere you are planted in changes the trajectory of your life. If a seed is planted in concrete, we never see it grow. But if we take that same seed and plant it in the right soil, it will flourish! God wants your life to flourish. You may need to relocate your life in the right place, surrounded by the right people who will help you flourish. Let us rise to be the men and women God created us to be. Let your light shine for all to see! Use your mouth and raise your hands. Speak all that God says you are! Speak and thank God for who He is and all that He has done.

If you prayed for something, and you had faith and trusted God, and He did it, have that same reassurance that if you are praying for something else, trust Him. Believe in Him. He will answer you again.

May you be strengthened by the Lord. May you be filled with His peace and allow His Word to transform your life. You will never be the same. And you won't regret it! And remember, tell your story and share your testimony with others so they may see how real God is!

Be blessed!

Building Bridges Ministry began in 2008, in my jail cell in Brazoria County Jail, the moment I surrendered my life over to God. I used prison as an opportunity for my relationship to grow in the Lord; I then began to minister to the other women who were incarcerated with me. I led them to the Lord, standing as a bridge so they could be reconnected to their Creator. Once I was released from prison, I was allowed back into the jails and prisons to minister with the Word of God, singing and sharing my testimony of how God changed my life. He has sent me back into the places He brought me out of: prison, jail, and the streets!

Building Bridges Ministry is made to rebuild, repair, and restore lives, strengthening each person with the Word of God by the power of the Holy Spirit, causing them to be the men and women God created them to be! His Word is mighty and can change the heart of any man or woman. As the Holy Spirit leads this ministry, men and women are being delivered and set free. Chains are being broken, and people are receiving the free gift of salvation. Men and women are being delivered from drugs and alcohol. Miracles are being done by the power of the Holy Spirit. The eyes of the lost are being opened and seeing the truth. We help victims of domestic violence, rape, drug addiction, alcoholism, depression, anxiety, anger, and unforgiveness. God is reaching many who are lost and blinded by homosexuality, rage, bitterness, and jealousy. He desires for us to be free… free of all the chains the enemy has a hold on us. As we share testimonies of what God has delivered us each from, more and more lives are being impacted. They are experiencing the same kind of freedom from Jesus Christ.

Building Bridges Ministry conducts many outreaches all over Texas, singing and sharing our testimonies. We are also involved in street ministry, taking God's Word and love to the streets of Texas, praying over people, singing, and speaking God's Word. We are inviting the lost to receive salvation today. We have many avenues of reaching people like distributing toys during Christmas to certain low-income areas and distributing backpacks, school supplies, and brand-new shoes for children going back to school. If you would like to be a part of these outreaches, you can donate and sow into our ministry to PO Box 1732, Alvin, Texas 77512. As you sow into our ministry, it is as though you are reaching all of these lives for Jesus yourself. Your love, prayers, and donations play a huge part in helping us reach lives for God's kingdom.

We are volunteer chaplains at several TDCJ units in Texas as well, taking God's Word and love into the very place He has prepared for them to finally give God an opportunity to change them.

Building Bridges Ministry truly believes that the enemy wants to destroy our families, homes, children, and marriages. So if we can teach men and women God's Word, our children in the world can be saved. Hurt people hurt people. And so as we help people connect with their Father, healing can take place then, causing their children to grow in the ways of the Lord.

It is never too late with God. We sometimes believe God could never forgive someone like us. But God can forgive, and He will. He loved us and loves us in our worst of sin. And when His Son, Jesus, was dying on the cross, He was thinking of you. The enemy wants us to have shame and guilt so that he can kill us in our sin, but Jesus said, "Come to Me, all you who are heavy laden and I will give you rest." Oh, you have a Father who loves you and will never reject you. He loves you just the way you are. He will never turn you away.

Building Bridges Ministry was created and designed to further God's kingdom for His glory. All the bad choices, mistakes, and regrets are never in vain; when we can share them with someone else and deposit God into their lives, that brings God glory! And we do what we do all for the honor and glory of God.

We are life builders, soul winners, and faith fighters!

We will be opening a women's home called Metamorphosis Transformation Home in Alvin, Texas. It will not be a rehab center or shelter. It will be a transformation home where they will change their lives forever. We offer a six-to-nine-month strict program for women to get strong in the Lord. Their lives will be healed and strengthen by His Word. They will learn the power they possess and how to use it. They will receive the knowledge of God in a deeper way and discover how to live a successful, healthy, and prosperous life.

You can find us on Facebook: Metamorphosis Women's Transformation Home. You can find us also on Facebook: Building Bridges Ministry. You can find me on Facebook: Trudy Nunez Montoya. Our YouTube page is Trudy Nunez Montoya.

For sending in donations/sowing/offerings, you can mail them to PO Box 1732, Alvin, Texas, 77512.

Feel free to write to us and let us know your testimony. I would love to hear how my book helped you or changed your life!

We greatly appreciate your support, prayers, and love. I pray that you fulfill the assignment God has given you and that you become all that God created you to be!

Your letters will be read and shared during church services or on the website. And your offerings and donations will help the lives of many people. Your seeds will help us provide all the necessary needs of these souls. Please label your giving, whether it be for Metamorphosis or Building Bridges so it can be placed correctly.

Me in one of our Custom G Body rides we use for ministry

Building Bridges Ministry is growing. The lives of women are being transformed.

IT'S NEVER TOO LATE

Building Bridges Ministry giving the Word
of God & toys to families in need

ABOUT THE AUTHOR

Trudy is a courageous woman who overcame all the obstacles that were before her. She was a young girl who at one time was confused and didn't know how or who to talk to about the things that were going on in her life, and so she ran. She was a girl who was looking for love and acceptance and protection. She is a woman who was challenged with dark issues and fell for them. She made many wrong choices and took her years to finally reach her end. And the moment she dropped to her knees, that was the start of a whole new path. It is awesome to see her walking in the Lord! It is evident that God is with her. She is walking in the purpose and plan God has set for her life. As she reads God's Word, you can see the growth taking place in her life. Not only is she standing on the blessings and promises of God, but she also encourages others to do the same. The presence of God is on her, and when she opens her mouth to sing, preach, and teach, it is like fire. She is a woman in love with Jesus, and you can see it! It is so encouraging.

Printed in the USA
CPSIA information can be obtained
at www.ICGtesting.com
LVHW040338030324
773357LV00001BA/238